PERMISSION TO GRIEVE

PERMISSION TO GRIEVE

PERMISSION TO GRIEVE

A JOURNEY FROM SIBLING LOSS TO RESTORED HOPE

Amy K. L. Busch

Love Over Fear, LLC
Highlands Ranch, Colorado

Copyright © 2020 by Amy K. L. Busch.

All rights reserved. No part of this publication may be reproduced, distributed or transmitted in any form or by any means, including photocopying, recording, or other electronic or mechanical methods, without the prior written permission of the publisher, except in the case of brief quotations embodied in critical reviews and certain other noncommercial uses permitted by copyright law.

Love Over Fear, LLC
Highlands Ranch, CO 80130

Permission to Grieve/ Amy K. L. Busch. —1st ed.
ISBN 9781736121702

TABLE OF CONTENTS

Introduction 9
My Story 15
    Before 17
    After 21
Validation of Grief 27
    Debunking the Myths Surrounding Grief 30
        Myth: Grief ends 30
        Myth: Grief is linear. 33
        Myth: Some people's grief is more deserved than that of others. 34
    Validation - Things to try 36
Honor the Struggle: Physical and Emotional Grief 39
    Physical Grief 40
    Emotional Grief 43
        Jealousy 43
        Guilt 47
        Anger - Do no harm, but take no shit 48
        Sadness 50
        Peace 52
    Emotional Grief Lessons 53
    Physical and Emotional Grief - Things to try 55
        Physical Grief 55
        Emotional Grief 57
Cultivate Relationships 61
    Relationships with Others Grieving 62
    Relationships with Those Not Grieving 66
    Relationships - Things to Try 68
Practice Self-Care 73
    Self-Compassion 74

- Self-care: Physical 75
- Self-care: Mental and Emotional 76
- Self-care: Honoring your Sibling 79
- Self-care: Forgiveness 84
- Self-Care: Things to try 86

Nurture Resilience 91
- Resilience: Things to Try 95

Final Thoughts 99

How to Help Someone who is Grieving 101

Afterword 109

Appendix A: Recommended Reading List 111
- Grief 111
- Resilience 112
- Afterlife 112
- Hope 113

Acknowledgments 115

About the Author 117

Dedication

For my fellow grieving siblings. I honor your struggle. Love never dies.

In memory of my dearest Dan and of all of the siblings we have lost.

PERMISSION TO GRIEVE

INTRODUCTION

"A sibling may be the sole keeper of one's core identity, the only person with the keys to one's unfettered, more fundamental self." – Marian Sandmaier

I am certainly not the first to notice, but it bears repeating: there is no word in the English language that classifies someone whose sibling has died. Spouses who lose their significant others become widows or widowers; children who lose parents become orphans; parents who lose children become childless. I became lonely. I became lost.

Dr. Kenneth Doka coined the term "disenfranchised grief" in the late 1980s. According to Doka, "Disenfranchised grief refers to losses that people have that aren't always acknowledged or validated or recognized by others. You can't publicly mourn those, receive social support or openly acknowledge these losses."[1] These people were not seen by society as worthy of time or support for grieving because the

---

[1] https://www.psychotherapy.net/interview/grief-counseling-doka#:~:text=Disenfranchised%20grief%20refers%20to%20losses,or%20openly%20acknowledge%20these%20losses.

relationship had already ended or was not seen as significant, such as an ex-spouse. Over the course of time however, other groups have been deemed disenfranchised, and siblings are one such group.

On the face of it, this seems like a strange idea. Siblings are part of the immediate family of the deceased. And yet, in my own experience, this is the absolute truth. When my younger brother, and only sibling, died at the age of 42, I was devastated. He left behind my parents, both in their early 70s, as well as a wife and two young daughters, ages 2 years old and 10 days old. Dan had been diagnosed with colon cancer at age 39, and he had been through surgery, chemo, remission, metastasis, another surgery, and then a slow decline as we sought any treatment that would cure him of the cancer that was ravaging his body.

As an empath, it was far too easy for me to put myself in the shoes of everyone around me. I could feel Dan's pain, both physical and emotional, as he grappled with the idea of leaving behind his wife and daughters. I could feel the anguish of my parents as they helplessly watched their youngest child and only son physically deteriorating before their eyes. I could feel the devastation and overwhelm of my sister-in-law as she cared for my brother and as she faced the possibility of a world where she would be the single parent to two children under the age of three. I could feel the struggle of my own children and my husband as they faced losing an uncle and a brother, and also watched me wrestle with the prospect of losing my brother and best friend. I could feel the sadness of our extended family members...aunts, uncles, cousins. I was touched by the outpouring of support and sadness from my brother's theatre and music families, people he had adopted as his own through years of performing. With all of the sadness, I was overwhelmed at the prospect of caring for everyone and exhausted by the mere idea of taking on their grief and struggle along with my own.

When Dan died, the worst fears of my life were realized. I lost my brother. I lost a big part of my past and my future, and unfortunately, I was stuck in a present that I didn't want to experience.

I was already inclined to do everything I could to support my sister-in-law; however, I was in a bizarre place of desiring to support her, but also trying not to step on her toes. She was, after all, Dan's wife. She was the one who was widowed with his passing and who was relegated to the life of a single-mother. Who was I to tell her how to handle his funeral and celebration of life? I was one of the first people to minimize and even invalidate my own grief in deference to her.

While I was quick to invalidate my own grief, I did not have to look far for others who would do the same. It was a common occurrence for me to interact with people whose first questions or statements were about my parents and my sister-in-law. "I can't imagine how hard this must be for your parents. How are they handling things?" "This must be so incredibly difficult for your sister-in-law and for Dan's girls. Is there anything I can do to help them?" "What a terrible tragedy. Your parents are lucky to have you to be of support to them." I felt like my grief was unseen and unimportant.

I was getting a clear message from society at large that my grief was less than that of other people. I felt guilty for feeling like I deserved a seat at the table of those grieving my baby brother.

As in any challenge I have encountered in life, my first inclination was to seek a book that would help me navigate these tumultuous waters I was trying to tread. I was stunned. My first search for sibling grief at my local library yielded one book, specifically for teens. My searches on Amazon yielded a list of many books about grief, but there were far more books about grieving the loss of a pet than a sibling, and the only books I found on my first search for sibling grief were books that were designed to help parents guide young children on their grief journey. As an adult sibling, I found very little.

The one book I did find was *Surviving the Death of a Sibling* by T.J. Wray. I ordered the book, and continued to search while I awaited its arrival. Why was there a hole in literature about this topic? According to US News: "Approximately 80 percent of Americans have at least one brother or sister; in fact, kids today are more likely to grow up with a sibling than a father, experts say. What's more, the sibling relationship is the longest relationship that most people will have in their lives."[2] According to the Centers for Disease Control, there were 2,813,503 deaths in the US in 2017.[3] Using those numbers, if 80% of those 2,813,503 people had at least one sibling, that means that, in 2017, there were at least 2,250,802 who lost a sibling, and we can assume that the number is much higher, as many people in the US come from families of more than 2 children. How is it possible that a group that size, a group that unfortunately grows every single day, is so underserved in the literature?

When Wray's book arrived, I opened it, and set it neatly on the shelf. As much as I wanted to read it, I wasn't ready. Dan's loss was too new, and daily activities were emotionally exhausting enough. Perhaps that is why it is an

---

[2] https://health.usnews.com/health-news/family-health/articles/2009/07/31/7-ways-your-siblings-may-have-shaped-you
[3] https://www.cdc.gov/nchs/fastats/deaths.htm

underserved topic. Maybe people prefer to, or are encouraged to, avoid or gloss over their grief when it comes to the death of their sibling. That had certainly been my experience. I was only Dan's sister. I didn't feel I had the right to grieve. That's what the comments of others led me to believe and to internalize.

Weeks later, when I was finally ready to read it, Wray's book was like a salve to my broken heart. She described in detail her excruciating experience in the wake of her brother's death. While I was heartbroken that she had experienced a loss similar to my own, I was also relieved to know that I was not alone in my grief. Reading her book validated my feelings of grief to some extent. At least I knew that my feelings were shared by others. It was enough to encourage me to seek help on the road to healing.

If you are reading this book, let me say that I am sorry for your loss. Grief sucks. Death sucks. The way our society approaches death is less than optimal for healing. That said, please know that you are not alone in your grief, and you are entitled to each and every feeling. Please know that your feelings are valid and you have a right to every one of them. It is my sincere hope that something in this book you are holding will speak to you and will be a salve to your broken heart. Nothing will make the loss ok, but together, step by step, we can help each other to learn to live with our losses, and hopefully, to find hope in life again.

PERMISSION TO GRIEVE

CHAPTER ONE

MY STORY

"But how can I learn to live in a world that doesn't include my brother? All my life, I've always been my brother's sister; it's part of my identity, part of who I am. My brother is part of my past; we share a common history. And we had plans for the future." – T.J. Wray

Shortly after we got married, my husband, Darren, and I experienced a number of losses. In a span of ten years, we lost six of our collective eight grandparents. Darren lost an aunt and an uncle. I lost a great-aunt. Grief is not a foreign experience. Those losses color my world even today.

I have had conversations with friends who have never experienced the death of a loved one. These friends have different hopes for their lives and for their children than I do. They express hopes for a certain career or level of achievement for their kids…for monetary achievement or societal recognition. My hopes are more survivalistic. I hope for health. I hope for longevity. I hope for happiness. How my children achieve those things is secondary.

When my grandparents were nearing the end of their days, and in the aftermath of each of their deaths, I watched my parents and their siblings. I watched them grieve. I watched them support each other. I watched them go through the planning of services, funerals, burials, cleaning out homes, reminiscing about their childhood moments. As I witnessed these moments, I realized what a gift a sibling could be in helping to shoulder the burdens of tough times.

We were nearing the time in our marriage where family planning was a frequent topic of conversation. I realized then that if we were going to have any children, I wanted to have at least two. I wanted my children to have a sibling to experience life with…the good times, yes, but also the tough times that every one of us faces in a lifetime.

We were fortunate enough to have two amazing children, and I was encouraged to watch their relationship grow. "Take care of each other," I would say. "You will always have each other."

Fast-forward 13 years, and I have realized that my thinking was flawed. There are no guarantees in life. My children are not guaranteed to have each other through their lives. I was not guaranteed to have my brother to lean on and to share joys and struggles with. Despite my hopes, and the best laid plans, I became an only child. I say this not because I no longer had a sibling, but simply because we no longer could help each other in the traditional sense. I couldn't call Dan on the phone to vent or celebrate. I couldn't meet him for a coffee and a chat about books, parenting, and family dynamics. He couldn't talk me off the wall when I was offended by family political rifts. I had to walk this path on my own.

As a big sister, four years his senior, I grew up feeling like Dan was my baby. As an older sister, I needed to be his protector. I am sure there were times when we were growing up when Dan would have preferred to have a little less "supervision" from his older sibling, but I took my responsibility very seriously. I was supposed to look out for him. We were a team. But I couldn't protect him from cancer. I couldn't save him and make it better. In some ways, I felt like I had failed in my duties as the older sibling. Wasn't I supposed to keep him safe?

There are moments in life that are life-altering. They define life into everything before the event and everything after. The death of my only sibling was one of those moments.

Before

When we were young, Danny, as we called him then, spent a lot of time performing for our family. He played his toy guitar and cracked jokes. He was always ready with a cringe-worthy pun or a well-timed punch line. A dear friend of mine from high school described Dan as "the perfect sitcom little brother." In my friend's words, "Dan knew how to roll with a joke."

Like many siblings, he could push my buttons quicker than just about anyone, and he could make me so angry. I remember the summer after I got my driver's license, my mom had asked me to take Dan to his tennis lesson. After multiple warnings that we needed to get going or we were going to be late, I headed out to the car and backed part of the way out of the garage…and sat…waiting for Dan to join me. After a couple of anxiety-ridden minutes of watching the clock, Dan opened the door from the house, his tennis racquet in one hand and his shoes in the other. He was NOT in a hurry. As soon as he closed the car door, I stepped on the gas to make up time. In the process, I managed to catch the corner of my front bumper on the side of the garage, bending it out at an unnatural angle. I stopped, clearly frustrated. With perfect, sitcom comedic timing, Dan looked at me and said, "Well, you know most accidents do happen close to home." Then he smiled. I could have strangled him. I now look back on this incident and laugh. He did have a way of making people smile and laugh.

Dan was a jokester. He always had a joke at the ready, and his laser-sharp mind was quick to find a pun in almost any situation. He also liked to do fun little things to annoy his older sister. Musicians will appreciate this one. While Dan and I were both in theatre and music, Dan was blessed with near-perfect pitch. Me…not so much. On road trips to visit our grandparents, we would sing along with the radio, and Dan would purposely hit a note that was just off…slightly sharp or slightly flat so as to pull me off key. He thought that was hilarious.

Another little brother thing he used to do was purposely shutdown my urge to sneeze. You know how sometimes you have a sneeze building? Dan used to see the signs of that building sneeze. He would step right in front of me to face me, and using all of his theatrical ability, he would pretend like he was building to a terrific sneeze. It killed my urge to sneeze…every time. He would then smile a big smile.

While our family didn't eat together nightly, the meals we did share together were never dull. Dan and I used to make faces at each other across the table. Then we would try to make a straight face…to remove all emotion and stare blankly at each other. The result, most times, was fits of laughter. It was a game of who could make the other laugh first. Childish, perhaps, but this game continued into adulthood. My children watched us engage in this game over Thanksgiving dinners. While into adulthood our meals together were much fewer and farther between, Dan could always make me laugh, and I relished the time that we spent together.

Dan was not perfect, but he was perfectly human. He was also exceedingly stubborn. I remember a family dinner during childhood, and I am guessing that Dan must have been about 8. I don't recall the exact culinary dish we were sharing, but I do recall that it contained water chestnuts. Dan, being the rather picky eater he was, decided that trying a water chestnut was not going to be on his agenda that evening. Now, Dan came by his stubbornness honestly…it may well have been genetic. My Dad and Dan squared off that night in what became known as the Great Water Chestnut Incident. I don't recall how long they sat there, but it was well over an hour. I don't believe Dan ever did try a water chestnut that night, but I suspect he didn't get dinner either. For years afterwards, we would laugh about the evil nature of the water chestnut. That said, Dan knew what he wanted and what he didn't want. Even in his last days, his stubborn streak was frequently on display. He was not ready to go, and he fought with everything he had to be here with his wife and his girls…to be alive.

As he got older, his love of music and performance continued to grow. In high school, Dan sang in an elite choir, performed in musicals, and worked with friends to record a couple of albums. He played multiple instruments, and when time came to attend college, Dan pursued a vocal performance major. He continued to pursue acting and performing as a career long after college. He performed at many of local and regional theatres in Denver and the surrounding areas, eventually taking on a number of leading roles, including roles at the Arvada Center, the Denver Center for the

Performing Arts, and his pinnacle performance as Don Quijote in **The Man of La Mancha** at the Lakewood Cultural Center.

Dan and I were a textbook example of the idea that birth order can be indicative of certain characteristics. As the first-born child, I was a high-achieving rule-follower and a responsible people pleaser. I went on to study hard, get married, find a sensible and stable corporate job and be a responsible adult in the most typical sense of the word. Dan, on the other hand, was the creative, free-spirit. He was less conservative in his pursuits and less financially responsible, and over the course of his life he often struggled to make ends meet as he continued to pursue his passions.

We were close as children, but since we were four years apart in age, and of different genders, we didn't share much in the way of interests, toys, or friends. He was, at times, the annoying little brother, and I was, at times, the bossy older sister. But, he was mine, and I was his. He was intelligent, witty, punny, complex, goofy, brooding, loving. He was my partner-in-crime growing up. He was my brother, my confidant, my competitor, and one of my dearest friends.

In adulthood, we lived very different lives. I worked my nine-to-five corporate job and worked with my husband to raise our young family. Dan worked during the day and then spent his evenings and weekends at rehearsals and performances. We didn't get to see each other frequently, but we always made time for each other. We traded phone calls, texts, and I attended every performance I could so I could see him live his passion.

In 2015, at age 39, Dan was diagnosed with Stage 3 Colon Cancer. However, despite the fear of cancer and fear of the unknown, Dan taught me a lot about courage. Through chemo treatments and pain, Dan continued to live a full life. He married the love of his life, he continued to perform on many a Denver-area stage, he made plans with his bride to add another child to their family, he finished a second bachelor's degree so he could earn more to support his family, he spent time with friends and family, he worked to move his family to a bigger house with room to grow, and he continued to choose love over fear every day. The daily act of continuing to move forward, to live life, was inspiring. Dan died in November of 2017, 4 days after his 42nd birthday.

After

Dan's Celebration of Life was held at the Arvada Center, on the very stage he had performed on many times in the years prior. The auditorium was packed, and many of his fellow musicians and actors performed or spoke. It was a magical and heart-breaking event. It was amazing to meet so many people who knew and loved my brother. It was amazing to hear the stories about the ways he had endeared himself to them by making each person feel special and feel heard. He had taken time to care for others and shared much of himself through his years in the theatre and music communities. He had so loved what he did, and he touched many lives during his short years on this earth.

It is tragic to lose a loved one any time. There are no exceptions. That said, that tragedy seems to be compounded when the person lost dies early in life. There is a cycle to life. Everyone will die; however, parents shouldn't out-live their children, and siblings should be with you into your later years.

There were so many things that changed for me after Dan died. They weren't day-to-day things. My world continued to spin. Work was still work. My kids still had homework, activities, and school. Dinners still had to be planned, laundry still had to be done, and the house still needed to be cleaned.

What changed was bigger than the day-to-day. It was fundamental to my identity. I was still a sister, yes, but I no longer had my childhood playmate, my baby brother, the one person who knew what it was like to grow up in my home with my parents. I no longer had the one person who shared my childhood memories. I couldn't call him up to say, "Do you remember when…?" I felt untethered. I felt lost. My identity in the world shifted. In practical terms, I was no longer the older sibling, but an only child.

Instead of focusing on and dealing with my own grief and identity loss after Dan's death, I immediately felt the push to care for everyone else…my sister-in-law, my mom, my dad, my children, my husband, my extended family. I had only known my sister-in-law a few years, and while I offered help, I didn't want to step on her toes. After all, she was now a widow with two children under the age of three…the youngest one only 10 days old the day my brother died.

Each day, I was more complicit in invalidating my own grief. I needed to be strong for everyone but me. I think this is common with grieving siblings. Yet, minimizing my grief didn't magically make it go away. In fact, there were days I was so heartbroken I didn't want to get out of bed. I hurt physically. My heart hurt. I couldn't imagine that I could move past this. My children, in their early teens, were accustomed to walking into a room and seeing me in tears. After a while, they stopped asking what was wrong, because they knew. Their hugs were some of the most healing moments I experienced.

My husband and my children were my primary support system. My employer and my colleagues were fantastic in their support of me as I grieved. I had some close friends who were there for me as I began my grieving process. However, from a family standpoint, I felt isolated. I was now the only living child. My parents turned inward and grieved together. My extended family rallied around my sister-in-law and my nieces. I felt alone, and I did everything I could to put one foot in front of the other.

I battled sadness and depression. While I would never have been able to take my own life, there were times when I wished I could close my eyes and the pain would end. I wanted to be with my brother. I wanted the weight of the responsibility to care for everyone else to cease. I wanted the guilt to end. I just wanted to sleep.

Based on discussions with many grieving siblings, I know that these feelings are not at all uncommon. I also know they are taboo to speak about. Society as a whole speaks clearly. Sibling loss is considered a lesser loss.

I was prepared to feel sadness when Dan died. I was prepared to grieve and struggle. I was prepared to feel the responsibility to care for everyone else. I was not prepared for the ripple effect that Dan's death would have on everything else in my life. I was not prepared for the far-reaching echoes that I would feel in every relationship, in every decision I made, and in the way I approached everything in my life.

Dan's death became the catalyst for me to explore everything I had done and was doing with my life. In comparison to him, I was the responsible one, with a stable job. I was the one who had followed what I was taught was the traditional path to success. What I realized was that my little brother – the one who at times struggled to make ends meet while he pursued his passion – had made such a terrific impact on so many lives. He had found success in his own way, and in doing so had brought light to the world. I struggled to say the same. It was losing this beautiful soul long before his time that encouraged me to examine every part of my life and to ask myself, "If I die tomorrow, will I be satisfied with who I am and how I have lived in this world?" The answer for me personally was "no." I have spent my life choosing to be who and what others expected me to be. I was an afterthought in my own life just like I was an afterthought in my grief. There is so much more that I want to do and so many more lives I want to positively impact.

Dan's death also created somewhat of a spiritual crisis for me. I grew up in the Lutheran Church, I have read the Bible cover to cover, and I considered myself someone with a relatively strong faith. Unfortunately, for me, the church felt less welcoming to me after Dan died. This was not because there weren't wonderful and supportive people at our church or that there weren't good programs to support people after loss. It wasn't even that my faith in God had been shaken. It was primarily that many of the platitudes that I had come to despise were repeated by my fellow church-goers more than by any other group I came in contact with:

- *God needed another angel.* REALLY?! God needed my brother more than my nieces and my sister-in-law needed him? More than my parents and I needed him?
- *Everything happens for a reason.* What is the reason that a 39-year-old man needs to get colon cancer?
- *It was God's will.* God willed my brother's death? Perhaps if I had prayed harder, God would have spared him?!
- *He's in a better place now.* Not even sure how to respond to this one.

- *At least...* There are a lot of versions of this one:
  ...you got to say good-bye.
  ...he lived a good life.
  To be clear, none of the above are a consolation to the person grieving. Dan is still gone, and I still want him back.

I still consider myself a person of faith, and I am still very spiritual. That said, I have not been able to attend church regularly since Dan died. I needed to grieve in my own way, away from the platitudes and sayings that were so painful to me early in my grief journey. Perhaps one day I will be able to return to church. We will see.

There are so many days when I wish desperately that I could reach out to Dan. Sometimes I miss him so much my heart hurts physically. He was one of my best friends, my confidants, my sounding boards, and my favorite comedians. I wish I could share the highs and challenges of parenting with him. I wish he was here to share the burdens and drama of politics, world pandemics, and everyday life. I miss our long conversations about philosophy over coffee. I miss his music, his laughter, his joy, and his hugs. He gave some of the best hugs.

I know Dan will always be with me, and at times I see or experience something, and I believe that he is winking at me from the great beyond. "Hey, Snooks," he says. I still talk to him.

I will never get over his death, and it will forever shape who I am and how I show up in the world. I will always be a sister, and I will always relish the times I had with Dan. I will spend the rest of my days on this earth keeping his memory alive through my words and actions.

I am working to show up in a way that will honor my baby brother and his life. I feel a deep need to make him proud and to carry on his legacy of helping others. I also have recognized that I need to be my own person, just like Dan was his own person. He marched to the beat of his own drummer, and I need to learn to do the same. For that lesson, I am grateful...but I would trade the lesson in a heartbeat to have Dan back.

I am thankful to say that the waves of grief these days are a little smaller and not quite as frequent. I still miss him enough that, at times, the loss takes my breath away. I will forever feel this hole in my heart. I am not ONLY his sibling. I AM his sibling. My grief is every bit as valid as everyone else's grief, as is the grief of every sibling who has ever lost a brother or a sister.

I was fortunate to have a very close relationship with Dan, but no matter what the relationship, whether it is close or estranged, an only sibling or one of many, every sibling relationship is impactful on our lives. Every sibling relationship deserves recognition when one sibling is grieving the loss of another. Everyone is entitled to his or her grief.

The following chapters include the biggest challenges I faced during my grief journey. At the end of each chapter is a list of suggestions or activities that were helpful to me. Additionally, I have included quotes from other grieving siblings. I would love to hear your experiences. What helped you? Please email me at amy@amybuschcoaching.com to share your thoughts.

CHAPTER 2

VALIDATION OF GRIEF

"We bereaved are not alone. We belong to the largest company in all the world--the company of those who have known suffering." – Helen Keller

First, as one who has struggled with feeling like my grief was not valid, let me validate your grief. It took me several years and many sessions with a grief counselor to learn that society wasn't going to validate my grief. I needed to be my own validation. I needed to give myself permission to feel what I was feeling and to do what I needed to do to care for myself, and I needed to do so without guilt.

Hopefully you have not experienced these same struggles in your grief journey, but if you have, let me offer the following: your grief is valid. Your feelings and your right to self-care are valid. You have permission to grieve. You have every right to be supported in your grief even as you may have to care for others who are also grieving. Your loss is not less than that of someone else; it is just different...and it is valid.

Second, I want to offer you assurance that you are not alone. I have personally spoken to many grieving siblings in the past few years, and I have been part of sibling grief groups with thousands of members. Unfortunately, the membership grows every single day.

> "My brother was the youngest of my 4 brothers, 17 years my junior (I am the oldest of the group). As the youngest, he was a bit of a spoilt brat but such a sweet boy and always had a lovely smile and a kind word for everyone. He was very charming and lovely and had many friends. We were as close as we could be with me having moved abroad when he was 5 years old. With the age gap, I guess I was in a way more like an aunt and a bit like a mother. We may not have spoken often, but the bond was strong and it was always lovely to see him.
>
> We drifted apart more when his life got taken over by the drugs that in the end proved his doom. He constantly tried to come back but addiction was too strong." - Ava S.

I am unsure why the sibling relationship is not more revered in society, especially when it comes to grief. The relationship with a sibling has the potential to be one of the longest relationships in a person's life. According to Dr. Heidi Horsley, "Most siblings will spend 80% to 100% of their lifetimes with their siblings on this earth... It is a really really big deal to lose a sibling. Very significant, but very unacknowledged."[4] Siblings are childhood playmates, competitors, friends, enemies, confidants, partners-in-crime, and the list goes on. Whether the relationship between siblings is close or strained, they have a great deal of shared history and the potential of a long-shared future as well. Why, then, do siblings fall into the category of "forgotten grievers?"

> *"We were born four and a half years apart. He was my only sibling. We were a very happy family with a great childhood filled with many wonderful memories. As we grew into teens we fought hard. I really disliked him much of the time. I always thought he was just so immature. As we grew into adults though, and got married and had children, we grew extremely close. So close that he and his family only lived about 3 miles away. Our parents were about 5 miles away from the both of us."* - Andrea A.

In the circle of life, we expect to lose parents, we pray never to lose children, and we hope to live long lives together with significant others...and siblings. Most siblings, however, are no longer living together when they achieve adulthood. Many have gone on to have families of their own. Siblings are also close in age, which means sibling loss can also cause one to think about their own mortality.

One thing I have learned for sure is that people shy away from anything that makes them think about mortality. I would venture to guess that sibling loss is one of the more difficult

---

[4] Mindfulness and Grief Podcast, Episode 26

losses for witnesses to separate themselves from. When someone loses a sibling, it is jarring, not only for that person, but for those around them. I think it is easier for many people to brush sibling grief under the rug than to face the realization that losing a sibling brings us one step closer to our own mortality.

It is my sincere hope that we can begin to change the way society views sibling grief. Perhaps we can begin to change that one person at a time.

Debunking the Myths Surrounding Grief

Myth: Grief ends.

I have encountered a number of people in my life, very well-meaning people, who have not experienced the loss of someone close to them. This blessing in their lives makes it difficult for them to relate to grief.

> *"They were supportive initially, expressing sympathy, but not much was said after that.*
> *"- Sarah W.*

I was at a school function for one of my daughters about a year after Dan died. It had been a particularly rough day grief-wise, and a friend asked me what was wrong. When I explained that I was having a tough day of missing my brother, she responded with, "I am sorry you are still dealing with that." I wasn't sure how to respond. What the uncensored, unhinged part of me wanted to yell was, "Of COURSE I am 'still' dealing with 'that.' Dan was my brother in life for 42 years, and he only died 12 months ago! And 'that' was the death of my only sibling and one of my best friends! I will 'still' be dealing with losing him forever. I will never 'get over' losing him!" Instead, what I said was, "Thanks."

Many researchers indicate that there is no specific timeline for grief. Everyone grieves differently. While we can learn to heal and grow after the death of a loved one, grief is not something that has a defined beginning, middle, and end. Instead, grief is something we learn to incorporate into our lives. It is something that may soften over time, but it will fundamentally change who we are. With effort and nurturing, we can begin to incorporate our grief into who we are and even allow our grief to help us to refine how we live to be better, more compassionate versions of ourselves. That said, we each need to grieve on our own terms and timeline. There is no prescriptive way to grieve, and we are each entitled to our feelings, even if expressing them makes others uncomfortable.

> *"I don't remember exact words but I remember feeling that something was wrong with me because I was grieving too long, too hard and too different." - Kaci B.*

Grief is an uncomfortable subject for many to talk about. And while it is frustrating for our grief to be misunderstood, we need to know that people are going to say the wrong things to us. They are going to misunderstand or say some of the cliché and hurtful platitudes that our society is famous for: "Everything happens for a reason." "He is in a better place." "God needed her in Heaven." Spoiler alert: these are not things people say to make YOU feel better. These are things that people say to make THEMSELVES feel better. Such platitudes are a way to rectify your loss in their minds and also to distance themselves from pain. They are also a way to quickly bring the conversation to a close. What more can be said? "I'm sorry for your loss. Everything happens for a reason."

> *"My relationship with my parents and some of my living brothers completely fell apart one year after my brother's death. My family is of the belief that grieving should be done in a certain way - and it's either their way or it's wrong. My mother was also very resentful and almost hateful, as she felt I did too well and smiled much too fast after my brother's death. He left us a letter where he begged us to make the best of life and remember him well. That's what I have worked hard to do, as well as to model for my boys the fact that you can learn to live with a loss like this." - Ava S.*

A friend of mine who is, very unfortunately, also a member of this club of sibling grievers that no one wants to join, said one of the most true and helpful things to me shortly after Dan died. She said, "Grief sucks. Just know that I am here with you to hold space for you to grieve for as long as it takes." She didn't try to hurry me along. She didn't say things will get better soon. She didn't try to change the subject. It was the most comforting thing anyone had said to me.

Grief can take months, or years, or decades to process. Dr. Alan Wolfelt explains grief this way, "Know this: mourners don't recover from grief. Instead, we become 'reconciled' to it. In other words, we learn to live with it and are forever changed by it."[5] Don't let yourself be bullied into thinking that you should be done grieving. There is no timeline.

Myth: Grief is linear.

When I lost several of my grandparents in close succession, I turned to literature to help me grieve. The first book I read was **On Death and Dying** by Elizabeth Küebler-Ross. In the book, Küebler-Ross outlines the five stages of grief based on her work with terminally-ill patients: denial, anger, bargaining, depression, and acceptance.[6] While these stages were not intended to be prescriptive, nor were they originally intended to describe the grief a loved-one might experience after loss, many people interpreted this as a linear movement through grief.

Grief for me has been less like a straight line and more like a tangled ball of yarn. While I believe I have experienced each of the stages of grief that Küebler-Ross outlined, there was no predictable progression for me. In fact, at times I feel like I was in several stages at once, and I have visited some of the stages many times. Just when I think I am done with the anger stage, something triggers me and drags me back in. In some ways, I think it helped me to realize that there is no linear progression, and there is no way to predict grief. Grief is not linear.

---

[5] https://www.centerforloss.com/2016/12/helping-heal-adult-sibling-dies/
[6] https://www.verywellmind.com/five-stages-of-grief-4175361

Myth: Some people's grief is more deserved than that of others.

I say this not to diminish the grief of anyone, but I do want to dispute the idea that the title of your relationship dictates the depth of grief. Each and every person has a right to the feelings he feels and to the support she needs, regardless of the relationship to the person deceased.

> "I felt support from my immediate family in those first few days. (parents/uncles/cousins). It really bothered me to have people always ask about my parents and sister-in-law. Like I didn't lose anything. I kept asking myself, "Don't people realize that I have known him for 38 years and always envisioned our families growing old together? I have lost my past AND my future. I'm the biggest loser here. And now I am an only child." I dread that question ever coming up by the way. I just hope I can keep myself together when it happens." - Andrea A.

Six months after Dan died, I attended a theatre performance. Some of Dan's fellow performers, people whom I had watched him perform with on the exact same stage, were performing in a humorous, almost goofy show. Despite my volatile emotions as I watched them do the very thing my little brother loved so much, I tried to enjoy the performance.

After the show, I waited around in the small lobby of the theatre in the hope that I might have the opportunity to congratulate a few of Dan's friends who had performed with him years earlier. I was able to say hello to a couple of them and to thank them for their performance. It was the last of Dan's friends to emerge from backstage who left me with a moment I will never forget.

When Lauren emerged, I hollered her name to get her attention. While we had met before, it had been several years, so I took a moment to reintroduce myself as Dan's older sister. She looked at me and started to cry. Of course she remembered me, she said. She cried as she reminisced about the time that she and Dan had spent working and playing together in previous productions. Then she stopped, and she apologized to me. She apologized for crying. She apologized because she said she didn't believe she should be crying when I had lost so much.

Here's the thing. Lauren had every right to cry, and I told her as much. She had every right to grieve, because Dan was her friend. In fact, her grief was soothing to me because she remembered Dan too, and she felt his loss was worthy of her tears and her sadness. I will forever be grateful to Lauren and for the valuable lesson she taught me. I recognized in that moment that her grief was no less valid than mine, it was just different.

I fully admit that I do not know what it is like to lose a child, and God-willing, I will never know that loss. I don't know what it is to lose a parent or a spouse. I do know what it is like to lose my only sibling, my grandparents, an aunt, a cousin, great-aunts and uncles, friends, and pets.

What I know is that, in each case, my grief was mine. Some losses were more profoundly felt than others based on my age at the time, the depth or closeness of my relationship with the person who died, and the circumstances surrounding the death. But all grief was valid for me and it had very little to do with how other people defined my relationship with the deceased.

There should be no hierarchy of grief, especially if it shames some into hiding their grief. The best way to manage grief is to feel grief, not to suppress it. While siblings are frequently classified as disenfranchised grievers, I believe that we can begin to shift this phenomenon, first, by supporting each other and second, by supporting those around us who are experiencing loss...no matter who died.

I see you. Your grief is valid. My grief is valid. Grief sucks, and I am sorry that this loss is part of our stories.

Validation - Things to try

Validation of my grief was a key piece for my healing. Some of the most beneficial things for me in working through this roadblock are listed below.

1. Join a Sibling Grief Support Group on Facebook.

    This was one of the most beneficial things I did in the early stages of my grief. Composed of people who have experienced sibling loss, this group became a safe place to share my own struggles and to listen to the stories of others. The stories can be raw and real, and there is a candor in the stories that is present because, despite differences in circumstances, everyone there shares a similar loss.

2. Find a grief group locally.

   Many hospices and places of worship have grief groups where people can go to share their grief and the related feelings.

3. Seek a grief counselor.

   There are many therapists who specialize in grief work. I visited a grief therapist for over a year, and the one-on-one support was very helpful. Many employers participate in Employee Assistance Programs (EAP) which may help cover the cost of a few visits. Other therapists are now offering online sessions.

   Seek articles or books on sibling grief.

   The most helpful book for me was *Surviving the Death of a Sibling* by T. J. Wray. For additional reading suggestions, please refer to Appendix A.

4. Seek artwork or create your own.

   There have been some artists who have captured the feelings of grief beautifully, and seeing the art can be cathartic and validating. (i.e. *Melancholy* by Albert Gyorgy and *Rising Cairn* by Celeste Roberge). Alternately, creating your own artwork can help in the healing process. It doesn't have to be pretty...neither is grief.

Things I have tried, things that have worked, and other notes

CHAPTER THREE

HONOR THE STRUGGLE: PHYSICAL AND EMOTIONAL GRIEF

"Deep grief sometimes is almost like a specific location, a coordinate on a map of time. When you are standing in that forest of sorrow, you cannot imagine that you could ever find your way to a better place. But if someone can assure you that they themselves have stood in that same place, and now have moved on, sometimes this will bring hope" – Elizabeth Gilbert

I believe that grief is a process. As I was searching for a definition of grief, I found the definitions in many dictionaries woefully inadequate. Perhaps this is because they were very technical and divorced from human feelings. The definitions also sounded static: "Grief: noun, keen mental suffering or distress over affliction or loss; sharp sorrow." [7] In my experience, grief is not static, but fluid. It is a process of loss, pain, and hopefully healing. It is also a unique process, because while it may have a definitive start, I do not believe that grief has a definitive end. There are many ways that grief can, and will, manifest for most people who experience loss, including both physical and emotional changes.

> "It's been 6 months since Joe died. I'm managing. But I still feel sad most of the time. I feel like I spend about 95% of my waking hours feeling sad but putting on a happy face. I talk to him a lot. It helps to feel like he's right here and I do feel like he is with me. It's some consolation."
> - Lillian T.

Physical Grief

Grief is a rollercoaster.

I remember when my mom called to give me an update on Dan's last surgery. He had fought through colon cancer to remission once, and now he had a mass. The surgery was to move the mass in his abdomen to reduce his pain. The result of the surgery was not what we had hoped. The mass could not be removed. The cancer had spread, and instead of the surgery solving Dan's pain, the doctor had determined that he couldn't do anything and had closed up the incision. My mom delivered the news to me by phone. "They are going to try to make him comfortable," she said. To say I was devastated would be a gross understatement.

---

[7] Dictionary.com

The next morning, I awoke at 3AM in a panic. How was I going to live without him? I was sobbing. I couldn't breathe. I was doubled over, and I felt nauseous. I was in a full-blown panic attack. I couldn't imagine how I was going to put one foot in front of the other. At this moment, my grief was real, raw, and completely overwhelming. This was the moment I knew I was losing him. Dan fought through nine more months of pain and treatments. During that time, I was trying to be hopeful, but I was also grieving.

Grief is exhausting...not just mentally and emotionally, but physically. There can absolutely be physical manifestations of grief, from exhaustion and sleeplessness to digestive issues, from headaches to a broken heart. Since Dan died, I have had moments of reflection and remembrance, sprinkled with laughter, tears, and love. Some days the grief is so raw it is hard to get out of bed. Some days the sadness and anger I feel are so pervasive that the best I can do is to retreat from those I love so I don't lash out. And then some days, the grief lifts a little, and I can breathe.

> *"That night, the police came to tell us Grant had taken his life in the hospital - everything surrounding that was particularly traumatic. I remember feeling ice cold and my left hand balled into a fist I couldn't open for hours. I completely fell apart and couldn't work for a few months. My boys were sick all the time that whole winter." -*
> *Ava S.*

Early on, my biggest struggles were exhaustion and headaches. Increased inflammation also made me achy. Some days, I felt like every step I took required a herculean effort. For me, physical symptoms were present for many months after Dan died.

My physical symptoms were exacerbated by the lack of time to truly care for myself. One of the challenges of losing a loved one is that no matter how expected or unexpected the loss is, I suspect none of us has scheduled time in life to take the grief in stride. When Dan died, one part of my life stopped, but the rest kept going. I had to try to incorporate time to grieve into the time required to do all of the other things that already filled my life: motherhood, marriage, family relationships and commitments, work, volunteer commitments, friendships…not to mention self-care, exercise, nutrition, sleep…. Sometimes I wanted to scream at the world, "STOP! STOP! Don't you realize that we are in crisis?! Don't you realize that we need time?!"

The stress and high levels of cortisol also contributed to my physical issues, and over the course of the first year of grief, my exhaustion continued as my weight increased. I couldn't find the energy to exercise. My eating habits were all over the place. Some days I couldn't eat. Other days sugar-laden carbs were the only thing I craved to numb my feelings.

Anxiety and depression were also present as I worked to navigate my first years after his death. Sometimes the anxiety was related to my health or the health of my children. I felt jittery and unsettled, like I couldn't stay still for any length of time. When the anxiety got bad, I would feel tingling down my arms or a sense of needing to expand my chest to combat the feeling of heaviness between my shoulders. Sometimes the source of the anxiety was hard to pinpoint. Overall, I just felt tired…so so tired.

Emotional Grief

In addition to the physical symptoms, the emotions of grief are as vast and varied as the colors in my favorite big box of crayons. My emotions ranged from deep despair and sadness to anger, jealousy, laughter, resentment, guilt, anxiety, peace, and everywhere in between. Some days my feelings would swing so wildly that I feared whiplash. At one moment, I might feel so sad my heart hurt, and then something would happen to remind me of Dan's quirky sense of humor, and I would laugh out loud. Then I would feel guilty for finding a moment of joy, then angry that he left me, and back to sadness. I felt peace knowing that he was no longer suffering, and jealousy that I had been left behind to care for all of the people in our lives who were missing him. As I said, grief is a rollercoaster.

> *"I have experienced random waves of emotions. About a month ago, I was at work and it hit me. I cried for hours and couldn't stop. It was to the point I almost had to go home. My husband tried to help but it didn't work. He doesn't know what to say or do. Since then I have just felt down. I cry in the car a lot too. -Kaci B.*

Jealousy

There are parts of grieving that no one discusses. They reflect some of the ugliest parts of the human experience, and yet, they are real. For me, jealousy was one of those parts of grief. I didn't expect jealousy to be part of my grieving experience, and I am embarrassed to admit that it was.

First, I need to say that I don't enjoy being the center of attention...at all. I enjoy my anonymity, and, as a confirmed introvert, I prefer to fade into the tapestry of life. Second, I am sure that my sister-in-law would have preferred not to be at the center of this perfect storm: a young mom and widow with a young toddler and an infant. Logically, I recognize that my needs for support were very different. I didn't have small children, and my husband was still by my side, supporting me every step of the way. I did not want to trade places with my sister-in-law, and I will forever be heartbroken that she found herself in this position. My sister-in-law needed support. She deserved support. In no way do I begrudge her the support she received. If I could have separated her experience from mine, I would have, and yet they were and are intertwined.

All of that logic aside, I was jealous of all of the attention my sister-in-law received. I watched as many well-meaning people flocked to her aid, financially, emotionally, physically, and in all other ways. My own family members who knew me since birth bent over backwards in an effort to support her. It is difficult for me to even type those words. They sound so childish and petty to my ears, and yet they represent true feelings.

My experience in the wake of Dan's death was very different from the outpouring of support I saw for my sister-in-law. I heard relative crickets. Many people sent me kind words of support on social media, and some of my close friends were pivotal in my ability to get through the last few years. And yet, many of the conversations I had with people in the last few years have started out with, "How is your sister-in-law?" I want to shout, "What about me? Why is it all about her? Don't you recognize that other people are hurting too?"

> *"I feel jealousy due to the fact that my sister-in-law has acquired a large sum of money from his death (life insurance, social security, and his corrections salary). It makes me mad that my sister-in-law got all this money from him dying. And I get nothing but memories that will fade over time. All of this happened during the time of COVID-19, which added another element to the mix. I was nervous about people coming to the funeral. There were lots of older adults there to support my parents and I worried about them at the time." - Andrea A.*

I recognize that hers is the more compelling story. Her situation tugs at the heartstrings. Her predicament is one that many would put at the top of their list of worst nightmares. I get it. I do. However, when someone reaches out to ask me to help them with the latest installment of "Let's see what wonderful thing I can do for your sister-in-law," it grates on me like nails on a chalkboard. I know they are well-meaning, but it further underscores my experience of cultural grief hierarchy. Some peoples' loss is recognized as more profound than others.

In addition to jealousy I felt over the lack of support, I was also jealous of Dan. That's probably something I shouldn't say, but I have spoken to enough grieving siblings to know I am not alone. Why did Dan bow out and leave me here to pick up the pieces? Why was it now my responsibility to keep putting one foot in front of the other, my pain so raw, while his pain and suffering was over?

I know, I know. He didn't choose to die, and I know, beyond a shadow of a doubt, that if he could still be here with his girls, it is where he would be. But his departure, though not at all by choice, left me feeling the overwhelming responsibility of being strong for my parents, my sister-in-law, my nieces. Without him, I feel like I must be the keeper of family history, ensuring that my nieces get to know their dad through stories and ongoing connection. I feel the responsibility of taking care of my mom and dad. And of staying healthy myself...can you imagine how hard it would be on my parents to lose both children? I can't allow that to happen!

But the truth of it is...I am tired. The weight of this responsibility, real or self-inflicted, on top of the responsibilities I already have taken on in my own life is beyond what I can handle. And yet, I don't feel I have a choice. At times the weight of the responsibility feels physical in nature...a heaviness in my chest, a weight on my shoulders and neck, a struggle to put one foot in front of the other. At times it is too much, and I let the waves of emotion overtake me...but not for long. I have too much responsibility on my shoulders to crumble...though at times, I wish I could.

> *Jessica described her feelings this way after losing her sister: "Deep sadness for her suffering and loss of what would have been. Guilt for not being able to do more for her. Jealousy of people who have a sister to share feelings and experiences. Finally, peace that she and her husband are reunited free of the terrible burdens of their lives." - Jessica B.*

Guilt

While I wanted to help my parents, my sister-in-law, my nieces, my children, my husband, my aunts and uncles, my cousins, and all of Dan's friends and support crew, and I tried, there simply wasn't enough of me to go around. It didn't take much time trying to support everyone else while trying to grieve myself before I reached down in the well of my energy reserves, and I found there was nothing to give. My inability to take care of everyone left me feeling guilty and inadequate.

To this day, I still struggle with guilt, wishing that I could have done more to help the other people in my life. In the early days of grief, I came very close to burnout. I was trying to live up to the expectations about the ways I was supposed to show up and to be of support for others. I still feel some residual tension about the things I did or didn't do to help the rest of my family. That said, at this point I have realized that there is a tremendous amount of wisdom in the direction they give in an airline pre-flight presentation: put on your own oxygen mask first before helping others. I was not giving myself any oxygen.

Part of my healing process has been to let that guilt go. I need to recognize and affirm that I did the best I could at the time and that there is no right way to do grief.

> *One of the most challenging parts of the grieving process has been "trying not to feel so guilty for not being able to help my sister more. I was her big sister and*

> *protector, but I couldn't change the course of the illness that ruined her life."* - Jessica B.

Anger - Do no harm, but take no shit

It is not surprising that anger is part of the grieving process. It is expected, and yet my experience with anger still caught me off-guard. Not the fact that I was angry, necessarily, but the fact that the anger was pervasive. In the first year after Dan died, I was angry...all the time...about everything.

For me, the anger was the most challenging part of grief. I experienced anger toward my brother for leaving. I experienced anger toward the other people he left behind. I was angry with the cancer for robbing us of an amazing man. I was angry at society for its discomfort with death. Our culture has a terrible habit of turning away from death. We speak in hushed tones about death. Instead of recognizing that death is part of life, we shy away, turn our heads, change the subject.

> *"I've never been a political person but my brother was a Republican and Trump supporter. I voted for Trump but I don't like him. After Trump was so lucky and privileged to have recovered from COVID-19 so quickly, his comments and actions really set me back. I was angry and emotional for over a week from a 30-second soundbite of him saying he's never felt better and we shouldn't let this virus control our lives and his overall flippant attitude. It was a huge slap in the face to*

the 210,000+ lives lost and all the grieving families. I hate that anyone can have that much of an impact on me with just a few words." - Lillian T.

There were big things to be angry about. Disagreements with family members about how to honor my brother, how to handle ceremonies, memorials, and his possessions were not uncommon. On each of these matters, I was trying to support my sister-in-law and to be strong for my parents. I was working to ensure that I did no harm while everyone was in a raw emotional state. That also meant that I was walking on eggshells. I was trying to walk the tightrope between offering help and staying out of the way, between expressing my opinions and overstepping my bounds, between deferring my grief to protect others and caring for myself. It was exhausting, and the result was anger and resentment.

There were even times I was angry at those trying to help. I was angry that I felt left out. I was angry that I was being included. I was angry that the sky was gray...and then I was angry that the sky was blue. Sometimes the things I felt angry about made me feel ashamed, but the anger, in some ways, was easier to feel than despair. After speaking with many other grieving siblings, I know I was not alone in these feelings of anger. Grief and anger went hand in hand, and at times I had to stop myself and ask what I was really angry about. Deep down, I knew that the blue sky shouldn't solicit feelings of anger.

During the months after Dan's death, after walking on eggshells and trying to be enough help without being a nuisance, all while trying to maintain my own busy life and to navigate my own grief journey, I was criticized for not being supportive enough to my sister-in-law. But who was supporting me? My do-no-harm strategy had not only failed to ensure I was there to support my family, but it left me feeling angry and oh so resentful.

> "I was very angry at my brother-in-law. The hospital told him my sister was going to die and he went home. That's it, just went home. Didn't call us." - Laura J.

Sadness

It goes without saying that sadness and despair have been part of my grief journey. Losing a sibling is so jarring. When Dan died, I lost not only my brother, but I also lost part of my past, I lost my present to grief, and I lost our future together. I also lost part of myself and my identity in the world.

> "Life is different, I miss talking to her, getting her advice, saying I love you. My heart aches at times because all I want to do is see her, hug her and even cry with her. Although she always told me not to cry! I am working on the relationships with my younger siblings, however we have a different bond. I miss her every day."
> - L.M.

Since he was my only sibling, Dan was the only person who could corroborate what it was like growing up in our home. In past years, I would frequently reach out to Dan to reminisce or to confirm my memory about a shared experience. "Do you remember when...?" is a question we often shared. The question allowed us both to confirm our experiences and the details that had started to fade with the passage of time. After speaking with other siblings, I am sure that we were not alone in this bond we shared regarding past experience. When I lost Dan, I lost the access to some of those shared experiences and the joy of reminiscing.

I also lost my present. I lost several years to grief. I lost joy. I lost my naiveté and my ability to look at the world with a view of optimism. Depression tainted my ability to be active in things I had previously enjoyed. I lost time.

> *"I am a quilter. I like sewing quilts and other sewn crafts. I used to sew every weekend and sometimes daily. Since my brother's death I have maybe sewn once or twice. I have upgraded my table and sewing room but haven't had the motivation to sew."* - Kaci B.

With regard to the future, there is deep sadness in knowing that the future I had envisioned with Dan by my side will no longer come to fruition. I will no longer be able to see him perform. We will no longer share those laughs over the holiday table. He will never call me to ask for parenting advice or to invite me to attend a school event for my beautiful nieces. He will not be by my side as I walk with my parents through their 70s and, God-willing, their 80s and beyond. He will not be with me to celebrate high school and college graduations, to attend band and orchestra concerts, weddings, funerals, and all that this life will bring. My future has been forever altered by his absence, and still today, this realization brings tears to my eyes.

Finally, I lost part of my identity when Dan died. Am I still an older sibling if my younger sibling is gone? Am I still a sibling at all? I have spoken to many grieving siblings, and one of the toughest questions for many is the question about family. "How many siblings do you have?" people ask. Many have pondered how to answer this question in the aftermath of sibling loss. Do I still say I have a brother? Do I say I had a brother, but he is deceased? Do I avoid the whole conversation and change the subject? This question of change in family placement, family relationships and family dynamics is one I wish was discussed more openly. I found deep sadness in the shifting sands of my position in the family, and I know I am not alone.

> *"I just miss him. I want him here so bad. On top of my own grief, I'm heartbroken for my parents who lost their son, my nephews who lost their dad, and my sister in law who lost her husband." - Lillian T.*

Peace

While it sounds strange, I did experience a sense of peace after Dan died. He had endured so much pain and discomfort in his last months of cancer, and there was some peace in knowing that his suffering had ended. Also, despite my pain and grief over his death, I also found peace in knowing that I had been his sister for forty-two amazing years of life. I am so thankful that he was part of my world and that we had been able to share so many moments, both good and bad, together. I am so incredibly thankful that I have photos, videos, and memories of our time together, because I am a better person for having known Dan.

> *"I felt sadness for my sister Kathryn's husband and for myself because we miss her so much, sadness for my other*

siblings, but peace because Kathryn had suffered so much with her illness and was no longer in pain." - Sarah W.

Emotional Grief Lessons

Through my rollercoaster of emotions, I have learned a number of things:

1. Grief can be surprising in the breadth of emotions. I have learned this is normal. Some people cry. Some people laugh. Some people lash out. Some people retreat. Sometimes many emotions hit all at once, and it is difficult to sort them out. Sometimes numbness prevails, and there is no emotion at all. In my experience, the best way to deal with the emotions has been to greet them as they come, and then to invite them to sit with me awhile. Pushing the emotions away was not effective for me. The only way to move past them was to sit with them, to feel them, and to move through them.

2. Everyone grieves differently. Differences in grief can lead to anger when everyone is in the highly emotional state of new grief. Each decision can create a ripple effect of additional hurt and anger. Some people want to grieve with others. Some people want to grieve alone. The best advice: "Do no harm, but take no shit." Choose empathy and kindness, but not to the detriment of your own health and well-being.

3. There were days when one thing felt ok to me, and then the next day I would feel differently. The best thing for me was just knowing that there were people I could turn to if I needed to chat or if I needed

support...but that's just me. Everyone is different. Overall I try not to allow my grief to push away those who try to help.

4. Everyone is entitled to their grief. Our society, unfortunately, has a grief ranking. If you are not the parent, or the spouse, or the child of the deceased, your grief is seen as less. I would argue that this ranking is not only hurtful, but diminishes the reality of human connection. It is not to say that losing a child, a spouse, or a parent are not some of the most challenging things anyone can experience in a lifetime; however, it is unnecessary to rank grief at all.

5. Anger can be pervasive, and it is often easier to deal with than hurt. Often anger is a mask for something else. Anger is usually pointed outward, and at times it is far easier to be angry at the driver who cuts you off in traffic than it is to sit down and to really face the feelings of sadness and despair that can accompany loss. Anger can also mask fear. Be gentle with yourself.

6. Sometimes it is hard to unravel the source of the anger. When emotions are raw, people may lash out at others. In fact, the anger may not be directed at the other person, but at the situation in general and the injustice of the loss. As the recipient of anger, I tried to put myself in the shoes of the person expressing the anger and to empathize. Alternatively, when I was the angry one, I tried to reflect on my feelings and where they were coming from before I expressed my anger in a way that I could not take back.

7. Self-care is a critical component of surviving a grief journey. While this is difficult for many grieving adult siblings who may be caring for a multitude of other people, it is important to make time for self-care. Offer yourself grace and the time to care for yourself first. Make sure you put your oxygen mask on before you help others.

Physical and Emotional Grief - Things to try

In addition to the suggestions listed on the Validation page, here are some things I found helpful in navigating the physical and emotional aspects of grief:

Physical Grief

1. Try to maintain a routine.

    Sleep can be pervasive or elusive when grieving. As difficult as it can be, establishing and maintaining a regular routine of meals, sleep times, and any other activities that you find enjoyable can be helpful in navigating physical grief.

2. Find moments of joy.

    It can be so difficult to experience joy in the midst of grief, and yet joy is an important reminder that there are things to look forward to and to cherish. The things you find joy in may change day to day, so ask yourself what will make you smile, even for a moment, and then allow yourself that moment.

3. Hydrate.

    It is amazing what some water can do for a body. I would recommend trying to drink a glass of water first thing in the morning and then with each meal. By linking it to your meal, it will be easier to remember.

4. Eat healthfully.

    As with hydration, taking care to focus on your nutrition when you can will be helpful. Increase fruits, vegetables, lean protein, fish, nuts, and seeds, and decrease sugar intake. It was very difficult for me to keep on a regular eating schedule, but eating healthfully when possible is a step in the right direction.

5. Exercise.

    Exercise produces endorphins, and "endorphins, which are structurally similar to the drug morphine, are considered natural painkillers...They can also help bring about feelings of euphoria and general well-being."[8]

6. Limit alcohol.

    Alcohol is a depressant, so while it might help to numb the feelings of grief, it will not improve things long-term.

---

[8] https://www.cnn.com/2016/01/13/health/endorphins-exercise-cause-happiness/index.html

7. Maintain connections with others.

    While there may be times you want to be alone, make an effort to stay in touch with others who can offer you love and support. Try to limit isolation.

Emotional Grief

1. Feel those feelings.

    In my experience, the quickest way through the emotion is to allow yourself to feel it. While it can be uncomfortable, sitting with the emotion when it comes up will reduce resistance and will help with the processing of your grief. Cry if needed. Get angry and vent if needed (preferably safely...by hitting a pillow or screaming out loud.) Laugh if inspired to do so. No emotions are bad or out-of-bounds for grief. Allow yourself the space and time to feel each emotion, hopefully when they came up, or at least shortly thereafter.

2. Journal or write a letter to your loved one.

    Some people find comfort in writing letters or writing down stories about those they have lost.

3. Write a "Fuck You" letter.

    This exercise is exactly what it sounds like. If you are experiencing anger, write a Fuck You letter. Rail against anything you are angry at: a person, disease, inconsiderate strangers, inconsiderate family members, death...whatever is pissing you off. DON'T SEND THAT LETTER! Once your letter is written, rip it into tiny pieces, crumple it up and throw it across the room, shred it, or burn it (safely).

4. Find a trusted friend who will sit with you when you need to talk.

   While you can also talk to a family member, sometimes it is easier to express all of the emotions to someone who is not also neck deep in the mourning process.

Things I have tried, things that have worked, and other notes

PERMISSION TO GRIEVE

CHAPTER FOUR

CULTIVATE RELATIONSHIPS

"Shared joy is a double joy; shared sorrow is half a sorrow." – Swedish Proverb

I know death is painful for those left behind, and I was prepared for the pain of loss I would feel. What I was not prepared for was the ripple effect that the loss would cause in virtually every relationship in my life. I think these changes were so jarring because they were unexpected. That ripple effect to my entire world was like adding salt to an open wound. I knew that Dan's death would fundamentally change my life, but I was blind to the way it would also change my own identity and therefore the relationships with everyone in my family.

Relationships with Others Grieving

I had only known my sister-in-law for a few years before Dan died. I loved her dearly, but I did not have much of a direct relationship with her. Dan was always in the middle. If we were going to get together, Dan and I chatted to make the arrangements. If there was a request for me to babysit, Dan was the one who reached out with the request. And while I enjoyed the time we spent together, my sister-in-law and I had never had the opportunity to spend any one-on-one time together.

This meant that when Dan died, she and I were thrust into a new and very different relationship than the one we had experienced previously. This new relationship, coupled with raw grief, made for some tumultuous months. I wanted so desperately to help. In fact, I felt an overwhelming responsibility to help, and yet we were just getting to know each other and learning to set our boundaries while simultaneously trying to walk through fire together. It was tough on both of us.

> *"I think the hardest part has been trying to support others in my family as grief is different for everyone and they go through the different phases of grief at different times. Having to go through all of his stuff and be executor of his will was very challenging as little frustrations would seem monumental to me at the time."*
> - Joni K.

I am happy to say that my sister-in-law has remarried. She met an amazing man who has stepped in to fill the role of husband and father to Dan's daughters. He is a blessing and a gift, and I am so thankful that they have each other. While at times it has been difficult for me to see someone else fulfill the role that Dan enjoyed more than anything else in life, my sister-in-law deserves happiness, and my nieces deserve a wonderful and present dad.

> "The last time I walked into my sister's home and knowing that it would most likely be the last was extremely hard. Her home was beautiful and all things Emma. She was an artist, and it shined in her home.
>
> I will never know where Emma's ashes are as her husband and children don't communicate with us about that. My family didn't even know the plan was for her to be cremated. My parents didn't say their last goodbye as there was no viewing.
>
> Her family started a foundation in her name, which is fantastic! It is very clear that her biological family is not included in the foundation. It would be nice to be included in honoring her. She was full of compassion and help anyway she could for those in need.
>
> As a biological sister, it would have been nice to have a piece of clothing, but that was never even a question or an offer from her family. We are the outsiders now!"
> - L. M.

My relationship with my parents also changed. I went from being the oldest of two to an only child, and I felt the weight of responsibility for my parents' grief support and for their care. My parents chose to grieve together, but whether they intended to shield me from their grief so as to not add to my suffering or whether they chose to do so because it was too painful to share, we did not grieve together. I felt very isolated and alone.

> "My mother wanted to do an interview on TV (which she did) and wanted the whole family to be filmed in the cemetery in that context. I explained that this was nothing I or my husband and boys wanted to do, but that we would fully support them if it was something they felt would help them.
>
> We tried to give them so many golden bridges, explaining our point of view (for me, grief is very personal, and I don't want to broadcast it on TV, but I understand that something like this can be therapeutic for others). In the end, they tried to force my/our hand at a family party, coercing, pushing..... It ended up with both of them screaming at me, and my father following me into a room, threatening me with bodily harm and telling me he would make me heed. It was extremely traumatic and threw me for a bad PTSD loop, which took months to get over.
>
> My boys both experienced the whole thing directly, and this triggered my eldest son´s suicidal ideation some weeks later. So I explained to my parents that I would pull myself back for a while, and I could not say

> *how long it might take to change that.*
> *- Ava S.*

Dan died in November, and just a month and a half later, my extended family convened for a holiday gathering. I really struggled with whether I should go. I was hurting and the last thing I felt like doing was putting on a "happy" face and gathering for what had, in the past, been a celebration. I wish I had listened to my own inner compass, because it was too soon for me to manage those emotions in a group setting. Again, I was trying to care for others without listening to my own needs. To make matters worse, there was the strain of trying to hold back tears. I was saddened that there was no tribute to Dan, no empty chair at the table, no mention of honoring the loss we were all feeling. I was angry and resentful. That said, I think many of us were on the verge of melting into a puddle of tears, so perhaps a tribute of some sort would have been too much to handle emotionally.

My extended family didn't deserve the anger and resentment I felt. They also had to bear the weight of Dan's death. Frankly, I was resentful that the world was trying to move forward without him and pretending that we weren't all forever changed by his death and the grief we were feeling.

> *"As her biological family, my parents and my siblings were supportive of each other. Emma's core family was very dismissive and still are to this day, despite all my efforts to connect and stay connected. I am confident this would be a disappointment to Emma. We are two years from her passing, and if I don't reach out to them, they don't reach out to us. Emma's biological children live 45*

> *minutes from my parents, and they have not gone and visited with my parents at all. Not even a simple text message."*
> *- L.M.*

The holiday experience caused me to isolate from my parents and my extended family a bit. I felt alone and unsupported, which turned into somewhat of a self-fulfilling prophecy. I was later reprimanded for not being more present for other family members and for not being of more support to my sister-in-law. Again, this caused me to feel angry and resentful. After all, I had been grieving on my own with little support from my birth family. Why was it my responsibility to support everyone else? While I know that responsibility was largely something I placed on my own shoulders, it was difficult to avoid the feelings of frustration when the efforts I was making were sighted as inadequate in the eyes of others.

Relationships with Those Not Grieving

In addition to the change in family dynamics, I was also surprised by the effects that grief had on some of my friendships. I had many friends offer love and support, and without some of those friendships, I would be in a much different place than I am today. There were some friends, however, who came to avoid me. While in the early days of my grief people didn't know what to say, as time went on, some people appeared to grow tired of my sadness.

> *"Three days later I finally posted on social media how I lost him (it took so long because I really didn't want to admit to myself it really happened). Once that*

> *happened I got many comments offering support. A few friends actually came to visit. A few surprised me because I did not expect that from them. It forever changed how I viewed them. Some I really expected to be more supportive, but I guess death can help you see others' true colors. I mean, I guess, I did read that some people are scared off by death. Who knows? "*
> *- Andrea A.*

Grief can be uncomfortable to witness. There are some people who are so uncomfortable with grief that they prefer to offer quick platitudes and then to distance themselves from the source of the sadness. As if death and grief might be contagious, they are quick to explain away loss, sometimes even assigning blame to the deceased ("He always was a heavy drinker."), or minimizing the death and feelings of loss ("How close could you have been since she lived out of state?") Every time I experienced such dismissals, I felt hurt and unsupported.

> *"People who were friends of my parents said that it was all part of God's plan. Similarly, someone sent a book written by a person who became disabled and then realized God was teaching her a lesson." - Jessica B.*

As time has passed, I have begun to see these responses to death and loss for what they are: fear. If it can happen to me, it can happen to them…unless they can find some way to distance themselves from my experience.

As I continue to move through my own grief, I encounter others who are newly grieving. I try to put myself in their shoes and to remember exactly how I felt in the early stages of grief. Even with my own experience so fresh in my mind, there are times I say or do something that feels less than perfectly supportive of the other person. I am human.

> *"I guess I try to remember that people often have trouble expressing themselves in that situation." - Sarah W.*

I would love to begin to change the societal conversation about grief and loss. Death is part of life, and we do everyone a disservice by speaking about it in hushed tones and by turning away from the discomfort of those experiencing loss. As a society, we need to allow those grieving to do so. We need to validate their losses and to help support them so that one day, when we are the ones grieving, we can do so openly and with the love and support we need.

Relationships - Things to Try

There were a couple of things that I would do differently if I were back at the beginning of my grief journey.

1. Reach out to family and friends to ask for support.

    Refusing to share my feelings with my family was a misguided effort to avoid further burdening them. This effort to be strong for them left me feeling alone, and at times, unsupported, angry, and resentful. They would gladly have helped if I had asked. I didn't.

2. Practice extreme self-care in the early days after your loss.

   While you may be taking care of others, don't neglect your own needs. If you need to sleep, find time to do so, even if it means asking for help. If you are not in the right place emotionally to attend a gathering, give yourself permission to say no.

3. Be prepared for uncomfortable conversations and feelings.

   I would have been better off if I had pursued uncomfortable conversations with my extended family as they arose rather than trying to tread lightly and "go with the flow" to minimize confrontation. Clearing the air as challenges emerged would have been uncomfortable in the short-term, but we would have avoided some of the smoldering anger and resentment that colors some of these relationships for me even today. Expect that grief is messy and relationships are messy. There will be challenges.

4. If need be, find a family counselor who can assist.

   Sometimes it is helpful to seek help from someone who can be objective. Navigating the way through grief is challenging and that challenge is exacerbated by the fact that everyone grieves differently. Do what you can to preserve relationships with the ones you love as you move through this grief process. One loss is enough.

5. If possible, talk about how you manage grief ahead of time.

    Not all deaths are predictable or expected. That said, if you have the opportunity to discuss how you will collectively manage grief ahead of time, you may avoid some of the pitfalls of trying to grieve together on the fly. I recently read a beautiful story of a group of sisters who were preparing to say goodbye to their mom after a long illness. The sisters knew, based on their personalities, that each one of them would approach grief a bit differently. They made a pact that they would be there to support each other despite their differences. This is a beautiful example of taking time to set expectations when the situation is less emotionally-charged.

6. Discuss expectations and negotiate something everyone can live with.

    One of my biggest regrets was assuming that I knew what someone else was expecting of me in this time of grief. If there is a question about someone's expectations of you or if you have expectations of someone else, open up a conversation. Their expectations may not be ones that you can meet, but through discussion, you can begin to work together to negotiate an agreed upon plan that everyone can live with. I assumed that my sister-in-law wanted more from me than I was able to give, given my family, my full-time career, and my already crazy schedule. However, since I didn't ask, I didn't truly know. Our road would have been much easier if we would have discussed our expectations of each other earlier in our grief journey together.

Things I have tried, things that have worked, and other notes

PERMISSION TO GRIEVE

CHAPTER FIVE

PRACTICE SELF-CARE

"When you say yes to others, make sure you are not saying no to yourself." – Paulo Coelho

I really didn't engage in self-care for months after Dan died. I took less than 2 weeks off, and I continued to do all of my normal activities, with grief and guilt added in for good measure. Beyond doing some extra sleeping, I was doing very little to carve out the space I needed to grieve.

The one thing I did do was to seek books on the subject of sibling loss. I needed to read about the experience of others to know that I was not alone. I hoped to learn about the way that others had survived the pain I was feeling and to feel the hope that comes from knowing that someone has walked this path before you and survived.

One of the things that amazed me as I stumbled through the early days and months of grief was the number of people I knew who had lost a sibling. Several coworkers shared with me that they, too, had lost a sibling. Others shared with me the grief they felt over the loss of a parent. It was evident, in the way people shared their stories, who had been deeply touched by loss. Those who understood loss were quick to say that they couldn't fully understand what I was experiencing, but they were there to hold space for me to grieve. We were part of a club to which no one wants membership.

As time went on, I realized that I needed to alter my coping strategies. I was not eating well. I was drinking more than was healthy. My exercise routine was spotty at best. I needed to begin tracking down some new strategies and resources to help me survive.

Self-Compassion

Dr. Kristin Neff, one of the leading researchers on the topic of Self-Compassion, has written several books on the importance of self-compassion. According to her website, self-compassion.org, she explains self-compassion this way: "Instead of just ignoring your pain with a 'stiff upper lip' mentality, you stop to tell yourself 'this is really difficult right now,' how can I comfort and care for myself in this moment?"[9]

Realizing that I needed to honor the struggle of my experience and to care for myself as I would care for one of my children or a best friend was eye-opening. I was well-versed in the "Grin and Bear it" way of moving through life, so the idea of self-compassion was new to me.

In her article, Dr. Neff describes three elements of self-compassion:
    1. Self-kindness vs. self-judgment

---

[9] https://self-compassion.org/the-three-elements-of-self-compassion-2/

2. Common humanity vs. isolation
3. Mindfulness vs. over-identification

As I began to offer myself self-compassion, I began to allow myself to feel the feelings of grief instead of trying to ignore them or to numb them. I believe this was one of the biggest steps toward hope during my journey.

> *"Allowing myself the occasional tearful "meltdown" when the sadness built up was helpful. Then I would return my focus to the present." - Sarah W.*

Self-care: Physical

As I continued to refine my strategies, one thing I did was to try to do something physical each day. Some days, something physical was as simple as stepping outside in the fresh air and walking a few-hundred feet, feeling the sun on my face. Some days, something physical was a more intense workout, even if it was only for 10-15 minutes. Each time I took a few minutes to do something active, I felt a little better.

> *"I found therapy very helpful. It ended up tackling a lot of other trauma, but it's been instrumental in my grieving process and recovery. I find walks in nature very helpful and photography. Ever since his death, my pictures have changed a bit and there is a notable focus on any kind of light. I also actively look for beauty in the little things.*

> *Yoga has helped me a lot as has mediation." - Ava S.*

My physical self-care also involved trying to do a little something each day to nutritionally support my health. Sometimes it was as simple as adding an extra veggie to a meal or remembering to take my vitamins. Focusing on hydration, reducing my alcohol intake, indulging in a healthy salad or limiting my junk food and sugar intake were other things that I did to care for me. One day at a time...one choice at a time.

> *"I grow flowers and plants and find peace in nature. I have taken on a new hobby, genealogy and enjoy the search and the stories of ancestors. Their struggles humble me and make me appreciate my own blessings. I practice yoga which is so good for my body and my mind."*
> *- Jessica B*

Self-care: Mental and Emotional

> *"I am doing better than before. I just try to take it one day at a time. Some days are harder than others. I am definitely not the same person I was before. I can't really explain how I am different. I just can tell that I am. I know that I look at the world and life differently." - Kaci B.*

Living in grief is difficult. Early on, each day when I opened my eyes and realized that my brother's death was reality and not a nightmare, I wished the day would just mercifully end so I could reenter the escape of slumber. Unfortunately, I still had a life to engage in and people to engage with, so sleeping my life away was not an option. As time went on, I realized that I needed to seek some additional coping mechanisms for my mental and emotional health as well.

There were a number of things that I did to seek support alone or with others:
- Alone:
    - I read books. (see list in Appendix A)
    - I wrote in my journal.
    - I cried…a lot.
    - I listened to music.
    - I tried meditation. (try the Mindfulness.com app)
    - I tried EFT (Emotional Freedom Technique) or "tapping" to reduce my anxiety.   (try the Tapping Solution app)
- With others:
    - I joined a Sibling Grief Support Group on Facebook.
    - I sought a grief counselor.
    - I reached out to my doctor to discuss antidepressants.
    - I reached out to family and friends.
    - I spoke to a life coach.

So many of the things above contributed to helping me navigate my grief. One of the things I realized early in my grief journey is that every day is different. Some days I needed to wallow in sad music. Other days, I wanted to journal or read. Still other days, I wanted to escape the sadness and just do something normal like watch a movie or go for a hike. Some days what I needed changed multiple times throughout the day. The approach I found most effective in navigating my grief was one of curiosity and experimentation. When I realized I was hurting and in need of some self-care, I tried to ask myself what I was in the mood for or what might help. I would try that and then reassess. Did I feel better? Was I ready to do something else?

Over time, I began to find my go-to activities for different moods. I began to recognize which things I could handle on my own and which challenges might require a conversation with someone else who could offer a new perspective. Google was frequently my friend as I searched for various resources in my area.

> *"For me, personal time was important, exercising, trying to do some restorative yoga and meditation have been helpful. I realize that there are times I just need that minute to breath."* - Joni K.

I spent some time with a grief counselor who helped me recognize that I needed to validate my own grief and who helped me work through some of the toughest moments of anger and guilt. I also spent some time with several different life coaches who helped me learn to believe in my dreams again and to plan a way forward. (Please feel free to reach out to me at amy@amybuschcoaching.com if I can be of assistance in helping you to find resources.)

Finally, and most importantly, I learned that it is ok to find moments of joy and laughter, even in grief. In the early months of grieving, my rare and fleeting moments of happiness would be quickly followed by guilt, as if in being happy I was not honoring Dan and the magnitude of his loss. After time though, I realized that finding moments of peace and joy in life were in no way a reflection of how much I miss Dan. In fact, the unexpected moments or memories that made me smile were just as important as the time I spent crying.

Self-care: Honoring your Sibling

One of the things I struggled with most was how to honor Dan. Since Dan was cremated, there was no grave to visit. There was a stone placed in a cremation memorial garden; however, the stone, which just said Dan's name, his birth and death dates, and the inscription "Husband, Father, Son" did not hold anything for me. In fact, because my relationship was not reflected on the stone, instead of being a place I could go to pay my respects, it was a place that reminded me that my relationship as Dan's sibling was viewed as less important. After some time, my parents chose to replace the original stone with one that was more inclusive of all of those who loved Dan. I do go visit it from time to time.

> *"I get my nails done every third week and I have my nail tech draw a thin grey line on one of my nails each time to symbolize my brother. (corrections is a grey line on the American flag). I also plan to get a tattoo soon to honor him. I'm struggling with what to get but hopefully something will come to me in the next year."* - Andrea A.

Depending upon your belief systems, some people find comfort in seeking a medium who can connect with their loved one. I did that too. I read several books by mediums, including Rebecca Rosen and Laura Lynne Jackson. I found comfort in the stories I read, and I relished the idea that Dan's beautiful spirit was still with me, even after death. I needed to know that he was still with me, and these books provided me with that hope.

> "I heard that my niece and nephew were in their backyard playing and were visited by a cardinal. Later that day I was also visited by a cardinal." - Kaci B.

A friend who loaned me some books by Rebecca Rosen invited me to attend a large-group reading in Denver. While I was still unsure what I believed, I was craving connection with Dan, and I agreed to go.

What I experienced convinced me that our loved ones are still with us. The reading was being held at a place I had never been to. As we drove there that evening, however, I realized that the location of the reading was a performance venue beneath a restaurant. It was a restaurant I had been to only once in my life. It was where I had met Dan for the last meal we had eaten out together before he died...just the two of us.

We entered the venue and settled in for the event. Rebecca came out on stage and explained her abilities before she got started. Then she would begin by explaining that she had a spirit with her who wanted to communicate. She would give a little information about the spirit to the audience, and based on the process of elimination and discussion with audience members, she would zero in on to whom the spirit's message was directed.

At one point, Rebecca mentioned that there was someone named Dan who was coming through to her. She zeroed in on me and did a reading about my Dan. She was spot on. She knew Dan's age and his manner of death. She told me about Dan's children without me offering any information about Dan's young family. She knew their ages and their genders. She told me things about Dan that no one would have known. She told me about things he liked, like his love for musical theatre and the video games he played with his best friend. She relayed his messages in a tone and manner that felt and sounded like Dan's words. She expressed Dan's gratitude for the outpouring of love that had been shared with his wife and children. I left in awe of her gift, and also in awe of the realization that Dan was still present, even if he was no longer here physically.

> *"It has been 14 years. I have an emotional time on her birthday in July and on the anniversary of her death in December. I know that she was not well. She was a sensitive soul, and maybe too sensitive for this world. I take comfort in knowing that I gave her love and joy. I am doing well. I think of her with love and fondness."*
> *- Laura J.*

After this experience, I honor Dan by recognizing the ways he is still with me. Through the literature I have read, some people connect the appearance of butterflies or birds with knowing their loved one is still present. I have experienced some moments where I feel his presence, and since Dan was a musician, many of those moments relate to music. I feel him with me when some of his favorite songs come on the radio or when I hear them in my life. At times, I will see his name in seemingly-random places, and it is a reminder that he is still in my heart.

Shortly after Dan died, we started experiencing odd things with the light and ceiling fan in our master bedroom. At times, the light turns on randomly, or the fan speeds up or slows down, or turns on by itself. We joke that this is Dan saying hello. When it happens now, I say hi to him. My husband will say hi to him too. Whether or not this is truly Dan's spirit reaching out to us, these unexplained electrical events are regular occurrences that remind me to connect with Dan.

> "Knowing that my brother has little tolerance for weakness makes me laugh sometimes even in my saddest moments. I think he'd be laughing at me telling me to get the hell up and move on. He taught me to be strong and I want to honor that."
> - Lillian T.

One thing I did several months after Dan died was to get a tattoo in his honor. Before he died, I asked Dan to write a word for me. The word I asked him to write was "Persevere." It is a word that holds deep meaning for me. It is a word that I have relied on to push me through some tough times and tough trials in my life. It is a word that I focused on in my quest to achieve my black belt in Taekwondo. While I sincerely hoped it was a word we would focus on together through his recovery, it is also a word I knew I would need as a reminder if I had to continue my life without him. Despite many requests, he procrastinated. I know for both of us it was a hard request. In some ways, it was acknowledgement of something we both knew was coming, but didn't want to face.

By the time he conceded to write it for me, he was weak and medicated. Even the act of him writing that one word for me was difficult, but it was an act of love. He wrote the first 6 letters, and then he couldn't focus on the task any more. It was as close as we would get. I took the letters he gave me, and by copying his handwriting, I finished the word for him. It seems fitting somehow. We finished it together. Dan's handwriting is now visible on the inside of my left wrist. As a tribute to him, I had the artist put it on a music staff, complete with repeat signs at the beginning and end of the word. It reminds me to keep going. It reminds me that he is still with me, pushing me forward. And on the days when I struggle the most, it is a reminder that when I have persevered, I must repeat. Over and over again. There is no end to the repeat.

My tattoo also reminds me that I am my own person, and that I need to express myself…to BE myself, just as Dan was himself. I don't have to fit into someone else's mold or idea of who I should be or how I should look. I need to remember that I am enough, just as I am, and that I can be happy, childish, quirky, introverted, quiet, resourceful, and persevering. I can also be loud, disciplined, confident, and creative.

> *"I have a photo of John, a fake memory candle and a daffodil from his funeral flowers (it's a fake one) that sits on a table in my kitchen. Not really a shrine, just a spot to keep him around. I do find it helps for me to talk to my children about my memories with him from our childhood. I'm still crying when I do tell them. I hope someday there will be no tears, only joy*

> and laughter when sharing stories. I'm not there yet though." - Andrea A.

I am still searching for ways to honor Dan and the place he holds in my heart. I have donated to some causes that were near and dear to his heart. I have connected to some of his friends and try to be present for them. I have attended theatre productions to support his fellow musicians and performers. I am still searching.

> "For me being able to go for a walk and go to the site where we scattered his ashes has been very helpful. Sometimes I go alone, sometimes with my husband or children and sometimes with my step mom who was very close to my brother. We have recently moved and left the state where his ashes were scattered. I had a canvas print made of a picture I had taken at the site. I now see it every morning and every night. It brings me great peace and a smile. I will still go to the site, just not as often but the canvas is so helpful! It allows me to center my thoughts and heal." - Joni K.

Self-care: Forgiveness

One of the most important steps in my self-care journey was the step of forgiveness. Grief is messy business. The raw emotions of grief after loss are complex, and that complexity only grows when multiple grieving people are trying to interact.

I felt so alone early in my grief, and I had plenty of anger to direct out into the world. I was angry at my sister-in-law for the way she chose to dispose of some of Dan's things. She was angry at me for not being present enough to support her. I was angry at my parents for not allowing me into their grief, and they expressed frustration with me for not being enough support to my sister-in-law. I was angry at Dan. I was angry at some of my extended family members for things said and done or not said and not done. I was angry at myself.

Grief is about loss...not only the loss of a loved one, but the change of relationships, the loss of control, the loss of normalcy, the loss of part of oneself. In order to heal, I needed to learn to forgive. The forgiveness was not always even communicated to others, because they might not have even known I was angry. Instead forgiving was an act I needed to do to release the feelings of anger and resentment. Everyone was hurting. Everyone was doing the best they could to put one foot in front of the other and to move forward. We were bound to step on each other's toes once in a while. I learned that the quicker I could empathize with those who were walking this path with me, and the quicker I could see their actions through the eyes of compassion and understanding, the quicker I would heal. I recommend forgiveness.

> *"My sister drank herself to death. I didn't know that the situation was so dire. For a long time, I blamed all of us for not knowing more, not helping her. But the truth is, each person in life has to be responsible for their own actions. I accept that I could not have saved her. But I can remember her fondly to her kids, think of*

> *her with love, and try to support the living." - Laura J.*

After some time and effort at daily actions of self-care, the waves of grief felt more manageable. I was able to breathe a little easier, and I found some tools that worked well for me. There were certainly ups and downs in this self-care journey. On the days when I struggled to make good choices or on the days when the pain and heartache of loss was overwhelming, I tried to refocus my efforts on self-compassion.

Self-Care: Things to try

There were many things I tried that were helpful as I was grieving. More than anything, I would encourage you to keep seeking solutions that work for you. Here are some things you might try:

1. Self-Compassion

    I would encourage you to visit self-compassion.org and to read one of Dr. Kristin Neff's books. Her work has been truly helpful on my journey as I learned to allow myself the space to feel my feelings and to honor the struggle of this grieving process.

2. Physical Self-Care

    o Talk a walk in outside or find a way to exercise that feels good to you.
    o Try yoga or another practice that can help you find balance.

- Limit alcohol and drug consumption, as well as other ways you may be avoiding your feelings.
- Seek to improve your nutrition, even if it is adding a vegetable a day or making simple swaps like a glass of water instead of a soda.
- Hydrate.
- Remember your vitamins and medications.
- Try to stick to a regular sleep schedule to avoid getting too little sleep or too much sleep.

3. Mental and Emotional Self-care

- Alone:
    - Read books, if that is helpful. There is a suggested reading list in Appendix A at the end of this book.
    - Write in a journal. You can write about your feelings. You can also write down stories about your sibling, both the good and the bad.
    - Feel your emotions as they come up, if possible. Cry, laugh, scream, or whatever you need to do to express your emotions and release them instead of keeping them bottled inside. If you have to suppress them to get through the work day, take time to sit with them later on...but not too much later.
    - Listen to music. Music is such a key part of the human experience. Listen to music that makes you happy. If you need a good cry, sometimes sad music is the perfect thing to help tears begin to flow and to remind us that sadness and suffering are part of the human experience. Listen to your sibling's favorite songs.

- Try meditation. An app I have found helpful is the Mindfulness App from Mindfulness.com. Additionally, if you have a subscription to Audible, there is an Audible Original called 21 Days of Meditation that I found helpful.
- Try EFT (Emotional Freedom Technique) or "tapping." An app I use, called The Tapping Solution, is free to download and will walk you through the tapping process, as well as some guided tapping meditations.
- With others:
  - Join a Sibling Grief Support Group on Facebook.
  - Seek out a grief counselor.
  - If you need extra support, don't hesitate to reach out to your doctor to discuss antidepressants.
  - Reach out to a trusted family member or friend.
  - Work with a life coach who can assist you to strategize next best steps to keep you moving forward and who can help you find things to look forward to as you continue your life journey

4. Honor your Sibling

Whether you were incredibly close with your sibling or whether there was strain in the relationship, finding a way to honor your sibling and to commemorate their life can be cathartic. Some ideas might be:
- Plant a tree in their honor.
- Visit one of their favorite places.
- Write your sibling a letter.

- Choose a way to celebrate their birthday that will be meaningful to you.
- Choose a way to honor their death that will be meaningful to you.
- Light a white candle at holiday gatherings to remember your sibling.
- Make a donation in your sibling's honor.
- Set up a small shelf in your home where you display pictures and cherished objects that remind you of your sibling.

5. Forgiveness

    If there is someone in your life you need to forgive, I encourage you to do so. Forgiveness does not mean condoning the actions of the other person. Instead forgiveness, defined as "a conscious, deliberate decision to release feelings of resentment or vengeance toward a person or group who has harmed you, regardless of whether they actually deserve your forgiveness,"[10] allows you to move out of the past so you can focus more fully on the present moment. Forgiveness allows you to move past the pain and anger so as to heal and to move forward with life. Grief can be so hard, and the ripple effect of pain can traverse a grieving family, leaving frustration and animosity in its wake. Forgiveness is key to releasing that anger so you can move forward in the present moment.

---

[10] https://greatergood.berkeley.edu/topic/forgiveness/definition

Things I have tried, things that have worked, and other notes

CHAPTER SIX

NURTURE RESILIENCE

"Courage doesn't always roar. Sometimes courage is the quiet voice at the end of the day saying 'I will try again tomorrow'." – Mary Anne Radmacher

I am a very sensitive person, and I feel things deeply. I remember feeling panicky shortly after September 11, 2001. As I felt the pain of all of those who had lost loved ones long before their time, I worried that my sensitive heart would never survive such a loss. I had endured a number of losses by that time in my life, and each one was incredibly painful; however, the magnitude of what was playing out in New York was overwhelming. In the days and weeks that followed, the truth of what had happened set in. I was not in control and tomorrow was not promised.

"I try to take it one day at a time and to control what I can. I concentrate on work, school and my family." - Kaci B.

I began to study resilience. How did some people bounce back after loss or trauma while others failed to recover? I wanted to know. I wanted to know what, if anything, I could do to become more resilient.

Resilience is defined as "the ability to withstand adversity and bounce back from difficult life events."[11] In my studies, I was excited to discover that resilience is something that can be fostered. Resilience is a muscle. Little did I know then that only 16 years later, I would have to draw on the resilience I had nurtured in a way I never expected.

When Dan died, I was lost. I certainly didn't feel resilient. In fact, there were days I just wanted to call it quits. I didn't want to live with the pain. But each day I woke up and focused on the reasons to get out of bed and to keep going. My children and my husband were my reasons. My puppies, the sunshine, and the possibility of making it through one more day were my reasons.

> "Friends and family tell me I am strong and resilient because I got through caring for my mother and sister and all the aftermath of their deaths and then breast cancer. I feel more that when difficulties arise, there is nothing to do but face them and survive. Maybe that is resilience. I try just to handle things as they arise and not avoid or hide from reality. I do feel hopeless at times, but I try to do what needs to be done every day, stay busy, and make time for the things I really enjoy." - Jessica B.

---

[11] https://www.everydayhealth.com/wellness/resilience/

A quick google search of psychological resilience will yield a plethora of information about resilience and how to nurture personal resilience. I read books and articles online. I took a personal resilience quiz which quizzed me on my reactions in the following areas: Composure, patience, optimism, gratitude, acceptance, kindness, sense of purpose, forgiveness, connection.[12] Then I developed a practice. Some days I was too deep in the depths of physical and emotional grief to do much, but on the days when I could muster the energy, I began to try to focus on some of the quiz areas where I had more opportunity to grow.

> *"My life has continued, I have started new habits of rising early for the quiet of the morning and focusing on what I will do to honor her with my thoughts and my actions daily." - L.M.*

I worked on fostering gratitude. On days when it was difficult to be grateful for much, I said a prayer of thanks for the roof over my head and the merciful close of another day so I could crawl into bed and seek sleep. Other days, I was grateful for the sunshine, for hugs from my husband and children, playing with our puppies, a walk through the trees, a job, a home, some food.

I worked on fostering optimism. When grieving, being able to see hope for the future is a big way to flex your resilience. According to Psychology Today, "People who are more optimistic have better pain management, improved immune and cardiovascular function, and greater physical

---

[12] https://www.everydayhealth.com/wellness/resilience/get-your-resilience-score

functioning. Optimism helps buffer the negative effects of physical illness and is associated with better health outcomes in general."[13]

I worked on fostering a sense of purpose. In the wake of Dan's death, I realized that there were goals I wasn't pursuing in my life. I wanted to make a positive impact on the lives of others, and I wanted to seek more joy in my day to day life. I wanted to break out of the day-to-day and to do something important with my one and only precious life. I decided to seek out opportunities to volunteer and to show kindness to others. Additionally, I decided to brainstorm ideas for projects I could work toward…projects that would help provide me with the sense of purpose that I needed to drag myself out of bed on the toughest mornings.

Finally, I worked on fostering a sense of acceptance…acceptance of my situation, my grief, and myself. While I was heartbroken that Dan was gone, I needed to learn to accept the situation as it was and not linger too long in the "might have been." I needed to honor the struggle of grief and all the challenges that came along with it. I needed to accept myself, in the moments I was at my best, and in the moments I was at my worst. I made an effort to practice patience in the moments when I was frustrated, when I was presented with a challenge, or when the waves of grief rolled over me.

> *"Self-compassion has helped as well as forgiveness. Acceptance and surrender to the situation as it is, while working to change anything I could and needed to*

---

[13] https://www.psychologytoday.com/us/basics/optimism

change. I practice gratitude and do my best to focus on good things around me rather than the negative. It is still ongoing work, but I do well." - Ava S.

My resilience practice is still a work in progress. Some days, I feel pretty good, and I am proud of the way that I have dealt with my grief. Some days, I need to offer myself grace and to recognize this will be a life-long learning opportunity.

Resilience: Things to Try

As mentioned above, there are many resources to offer suggestions for building resilience so you can learn to bounce back more quickly after loss, trauma, or challenge. People who are highly resilient are not any less likely to encounter loss, they are just better able to cope and to regain their footing.

It is my hope that some of the suggestions below may help you to nurture resilience. Some things to try are:

1. Practice Resilience

    Find one or two small steps you can take toward a more resilient you. Ideas might be:
    a. Practice Gratitude - each day write down at least three things you are grateful for. Bonus if you can find three things each morning and three things before bed.
    b. Practice Kindness - be patient and kind with those around you. Be patient and kind with yourself. Make an effort to do something nice for a friend, a loved one, or even a

stranger. Even a warm and authentic smile can brighten the recipient's day...and yours too.

    c. Brainstorm projects that will give you a sense of purpose. Do you want to volunteer? Do you have a bucket list project that gives you a feeling of excitement and joy? I decided to make it my goal to help other grieving siblings. Is there something that you want to do? What is one small step you can take toward making your idea a reality?

    d. Flex your hope muscle - Look around. What can you see that gives you a sense of hope about the future? Growing flowers? Birds? Children?

2. Gentle Reminders

    Set up reminders on your phone to practice your chosen resilient steps. Do your best, which can fluctuate on any given day.

3. Read about resilience

    Google "psychological resilience" or search "resilience" where you buy books or at your local library. There are many articles and books that have step by step ideas to help you cultivate high resilience. Find one that speaks to you.

4. Take turtle steps.

    This is an opportunity for lifetime practice. Once you feel like you have mastered one resilience skill, consider practicing another.

Things I have tried, things that have worked, and other notes

PERMISSION TO GRIEVE

CHAPTER SEVEN

FINAL THOUGHTS

I offered many suggestions of things to try which may help you as you navigate your grief journey. Allow me to offer one more suggestion: please take what speaks to you from the previous pages and give yourself permission to let go of the rest. Pick one or two things that resonate with you and experiment with a spirit of curiosity. If you feel like something is helpful, great. If not, allow yourself to try something else. Most importantly, I encourage you to continue to take steps forward. Continue to allow yourself to feel the feelings and to put one foot in front of the other. One day at a time. One breath at a time.

I am only three years into my sibling grief journey. I have spoken to many siblings who are ahead of me on their journeys, and based on those discussions, I know I will never be done grieving; however, I have also been reassured that it will get easier. The sharp edges of grief can soften with time, and the waves of grief will get smaller and more predictable. It is my sincere hope that you have found something healing in these pages. As a member of this club none of us ever wanted to join, I want you to know that I see you. I honor your struggle.

I would love to hear from you. Please reach out to me at amybuschcoaching.com to share stories of your sibling and to let me know how you are progressing on your grief journey. I wish you healing and peace.

CHAPTER EIGHT

HOW TO HELP SOMEONE WHO IS GRIEVING

I would argue this is a skill that everyone should learn since, unfortunately, everyone will experience loss at some point. Unfortunately, since everyone grieves differently, there is no one correct way to support someone who is grieving. I have heard some people grieving say, "Don't ask me what I need. Just show up and do something to help." I have heard other grieving people say, "I wish someone would just ask me what I needed instead of trying to guess." Not only does grief change person to person, it also changes day to day.

For those who have not experienced the death of a loved one, it is difficult to know what to say or what to do to help those who are grieving. Even for those of us who have grieved, it can be difficult to know what to say. I can only speak for my experience. What I can tell you is this: There is no time limit on grief. It is not a linear process, and there is no defined end. It doesn't resolve. My life has been transformed into two parts: the before and the after.

> *"Reach out often and in small ways. Send a text, a card, a meal. But do it for a year, or two years. Not just the first 2 months after the death. Don't ask for details. If you have photos of the person, give them to the one who is grieving - make copies if you want to keep your own. Say their name to the one who is grieving. Not just 'sorry about your sister' but 'sorry about the loss of Katie.' "* - Laura J.

Recognizing that this is a burden I will bear until I take my last breath, I have learned some things that have helped me navigate grief so far. Based on my experiences of both personal grief and of supporting friends and loved ones who are grieving, here are some suggestions of things to try if you find yourself trying to support someone who is grieving:

1. Grieving takes time and space.

    The grieving person may not need anything specific in any given moment, but knowing that there are people who will listen is critical, even if they need to tell the same story about their loved one they have told before.

    > *"Check in on them regularly, offer a date to meet up to talk, ask about your past memories of/with them. Don't say stupid things like, "at least they are no longer suffering" or "they are in a better place" or "he/she/they wouldn't want you sitting here crying, they would want to see you happy and enjoying life". People grieve differently, and how ever they do it is their path. No one can say it's right or wrong. If*

> *the grieving process is interfering with daily responsibilities or not allowing you to enjoy things you once did, then is time to talk to someone: family doctor or therapist. Suffering should not beget more suffering. Suffering should produce more kindness in our world. "* - Andrea A.

2. Encourage them to make time to feel the feelings.

    The best way through grief is to feel the feelings and to work through them instead of pushing them away. Sometimes sharing these thoughts and feelings with someone can be instrumental in healing.

    > *"Just be there. You don't need to say anything. The most amazing help I got was from a colleague, who just sat with me for over an hour and held my hand while I helplessly cried. And then she went and found numbers and contacts for me to set up an emergency session with a therapist and told me I needed to go and just focus on letting go and getting better (the perfectionist in me was still trying to hold everything together and make work function)."* - Ava S.

3. There will be ups and downs.

    I read a description that compared grief to the waves of the ocean. As time passes, it gets a little easier to predict the waves (holidays, birthdays, anniversaries, etc.) Sometimes there is a rogue wave that comes from nowhere. Since Dan was a musician, I am regularly triggered by songs that remind me of him. I have learned that it is important to feel these feelings when they arise. Only by validating the feelings and by sitting with them do they begin to soften.

4. Just because the person who died is no longer here physically doesn't mean the relationship is over.

    It is important to continue to honor the deceased and the relationship with them by speaking about them when it is natural to do so. Perhaps encourage the griever to continue to chat with their lost loved one, to write to them, and to feel their presence.

5. Don't be offended. Keep trying.

    If you are offering help, keep trying and don't get offended if the grieving person is less than receptive. Sometimes it is difficult to know what will help, and sometimes nothing will. Let the griever know that you are available and that you are there for them. Check in on them regularly. Just because they don't reach out doesn't mean they don't need you.

> "I would say to step up. If you see someone isn't reaching out to you or asking for help, just show up or ask them how they are really doing. I have not had one person ask me how I am doing with my brother's death, not one. I am having a really hard time, and I am not the type to reach out. So I need someone to come to me, and I don't think I am alone in feeling like that." - Kaci B.

6. Don't hesitate to say the name of the deceased loved one.

   I have heard more than one person say they didn't want to remind their grieving friend of the loss. You can certainly ask the griever if it is an ok time to talk about their loved one, but the truth of the matter is that you are not reminding them of the loss. They didn't forget. In my case, the reality of Dan's absence is with me from the moment I wake until the moment I fall asleep. In fact, instead of being a burden, it is a relief to me when someone says Dan's name, tells me a story about him, or asks me to talk about him. Even if tears begin to flow, it is cathartic to be able to say his name out loud and to know that someone else remembers him. Talking about him is a way to honor his memory and to keep him alive in my heart and mind.

   "Just be there. And talk about the person they lost and never change the subject to avoid sadness. "- Lillian T.

   "Acknowledge the pain. Don't say "let me know if you need anything". Observe and do things that are helpful. Offer an outing for change of pace. Babysit, if that is needed. Speak of good memories of their loved one. Keep making contact after the initial grieving period. Don't expect the person to 'snap out of it'; grieving takes time and really never ends, it just becomes less painful with time." - Jessica B.

For those who shy away because death is hard and because it is hard to know what to say, I will tell you that one of the most helpful messages I received in the wake of Dan's death was a card from a friend. Instead of sugary platitudes about Dan being in a better place (which is an AWFUL thing to read), this card simply read, "This really sucks. I am sorry this loss is part of your story. I am here to hold space for you while you grieve." Sometimes words can be woefully insufficient, but just knowing that someone recognizes the pain, and is willing to sit with you through it, can be the greatest gift of all.

> *"Be there, listen, and keep asking if they can help, months, years later, everyone is different in what and when their needs are. Listening to them and not projecting what you think you would need is very helpful."*
> *- Joni K.*

So...for all of those who are grieving, and whether the loss is recent or years old, let me say, "This really sucks, and I am sorry this loss is part of your story. I am here to hold space for you while you grieve. May your loved one's memory be a blessing."

Things I have tried, things that have worked, and other notes

PERMISSION TO GRIEVE

CONCLUSION

Just because Dan is not here physically doesn't mean our relationship is over. Dan will always be my brother. He will always be a treasured part of my life. I need to honor that relationship by speaking about him when it is natural to do so. I have continued to chat with him, to write to him, and to feel his presence. I welcome others to continue to do the same. For those who knew him, I welcome you to share your stories of Dan with me. Never hesitate to speak his name. It is through this remembrance, and through the lives of his beautiful little girls, that his legacy continues.

PERMISSION TO GRIEVE

APPENDIX A: RECOMMENDED READING LIST

Grief

Surviving the Death of a Sibling: Living Through Grief When an Adult Brother or Sister Dies by T. J. Wray

On Grief and Grieving: Finding the Meaning of Grief Through the Five Stages of Loss by Elisabeth Kübler-Ross (Author), David Kessler (Author)

The Empty Room: Understanding Sibling Loss by Elizabeth DeVita-Raeburn

Everything Happens for a Reason: And Other Lies I've Loved by Kate Bowler

More Beautiful Than Before: How Suffering Transforms Us by Steve Leder

A Grief Observed by C.S. Lewis

Grief Is a Journey: Finding Your Path Through Loss by Dr. Kenneth Doka

It's OK That You're Not OK: Meeting Grief and Loss in a Culture That Doesn't Understand by Megan Devine

Resilience

Self-Compassion: The Proven Power of Being Kind to Yourself by Kristin Neff

Self-Compassion Step by Step: The Proven Power of Being Kind to Yourself by Kristin Neff

Resilience: Powerful Practices for Bouncing Back from Disappointment, Difficulty, and Even Disaster by Linda Graham

The Resilience Breakthrough: 27 Tools for Turning Adversity into Action by Christian Moore

Afterlife

Spirited: Unlock Your Psychic Self and Change Your Life by Rebecca Rosen (February 22, 2011)

Awaken the Spirit Within: 10 Steps to Ignite Your Life and Fulfill Your Divine Purpose by Rebecca Rosen

What the Dead Have Taught Me About Living Well by Rebecca Rosen

Signs: The Secret Language of the Universe by Laura Lynne Jackson

The Light Between Us: Stories from Heaven. Lessons for the Living by Laura Lynne Jackson

Hope

The Book of Joy: Lasting Happiness in a Changing World By Dalai Lama and Desmond Tutu

PERMISSION TO GRIEVE

ACKNOWLEDGMENTS

I want to thank those people in my life who have been instrumental in my healing journey:

To Darren, Riley, and Lindsey – I love each of you so much! Thank you for being the best husband and children I could ever have asked for. I am so thankful for your undying love, support, and endless hugs.

To my parents, Charlie and Jeannie, thank you for your love and support through the years. I am so grateful! I love you both so much.

To my amazing parents-in-law, Dave and Kathy - I am so incredibly blessed to be able to call you Dad and Mom. Thank you for welcoming me into your family and into your hearts. I love you both!

To my family—Austinn, Ben, Brian, Frank, Jill, Joe, Joni, Kaitlin, Marilee, Sandi, Taylor - I love you all. Thank you for walking this adventure of life with me.

To Rebecca and Fletcher - I love you both, and I wish you many years of happiness and love!

To Clara and Naomi - Your Daddy loved you so much. Please know that he is always with you. I love you both very much, and I look forward to sharing stories of your Daddy with you!

To the Joseph family - Thank you for everything you did for Dan in his last years and for all of the ways you continue to share his legacy with his children.

To my friends and friends of Dan - Alanna, Alison, Anna, Colleen, Dawn, Deena, Elena, Eric, Jennifer, Judy, Kristi, Lani, Lauren, Linda, Marianne, Mary, Megan, Patience, Randy, Regina, Robin, Samantha, Shannon, Shelley, Sonya, Svanhvit, Tammy, Tiffany, Tommie Jean, Traci, and Troy and so many others who I have not named here explicitly - Thank you for sharing your love and support and for sharing your hugs, tears, and memories of Dan with me.

To Kristi, Mary, Robin, and Tommie Jean - thank you for your editing help!

To Andrea, Joni, Kaci, Lillian, and the others who shared your sibling grief stories with me. I am forever grateful and wish you healing, peace, much love, and hope.

To my one and only sibling, my brother Dan, I miss you every single day. This is for you.

ABOUT THE AUTHOR

Amy K. L. Busch is a life coach, a writer, and the founder of amybuschcoaching.com. Her mission is to help those who have experienced loss navigate and thrive through change by applying change management techniques she uses in her corporate world of software development. She holds a Masters of Information Systems and a Masters of Business Administration from the University of Colorado at Denver, and is an avid life-long learner. She lives in Denver, Colorado with her incredibly supportive husband, two amazing children, and two adorable dogs.

www.ingramcontent.com/pod-product-compliance
Lightning Source LLC
Chambersburg PA
CBHW072204100526
44589CB00015B/2367